ULTIMATE GUIDE TO BUYING YOUR HOME

Insider Secrets from the Nation's Top Agents

Foreword by **TODD TRAMONTE**

Copyright © 2022
All Rights Reserved

 REGS Publishing
Dallas, TX

ISBN: 978-1-64649-257-2 (print)
ISBN: 978-1-64649-258-9 (ebook)
ISBN: 978-1-64649-259-6 (hardcover)

No part of this publication may be reproduced, distributed, or transmitted in any form or by any means, including photocopying, recording, or other electronic or mechanical methods, without the prior written permission of the author, except in the case of brief quotations embodied in critical reviews and certain other noncommercial uses permitted by copyright law.

All proceeds from the sale of this book go to feed, clothe, and educate children in need around the globe.

Printed in the United States

CONTENTS

Foreword: The American Dream
Todd Tramonte 1

The Power of Cash
Andrew Smith 5

Old Homes for Better Value
Brandon Wyatt 17

Finding a House for Retirement
Dino DiNenna 27

Writing an Offer to Get the House You Really Want
Joelle Dowe 35

Buying & Selling Simultaneously
John Byers... 49

How to Win Big Before Your Start
Leah Littenberg.. 63

Buying a Second Home in a Lifestyle or Destination Market
Garrett & Donna Sandell 75

Secret and Successful Negotiating Strategies
Leslie Stewart... 83

What You Need to Know When It Comes to Buying New Construction
Mari Arstein 93

Institutional Investing
Michael Oden 107

Buyer's Mindset
Rawlins Goldston 119

Buying Like a Celebrity
Brian Witt 129

Building Your Waterfront Timeline
Stephanie Jones 137

Building Wealth Through Real Estate
Matthew Patterson 147

Why Relationships Matter
David Goss 159

FOREWORD

THE AMERICAN DREAM

Buying a home should be one of the most joyous occasions in your life. This is, however, all too often not the case.

It was the summer of 2006 when I heard probably the best company slogan ever. I'm not a huge fan of slogans, but this one grabbed me. I was baking my brains on a hot Texas day with a buddy in some decent seats behind home plate watching the Texas Rangers play at Ameriquest Field. The announcer seemed more proud to read his promotional note than normal when he said, "Proud sponsor of the American dream!"

I thought to myself, "Me too." I am a proud sponsor of the American dream, as are a select few real estate agents and brokers across this great country.

Ironically, Ameriquest Mortgage Company would be out of business barely more than a year later and their naming rights deal with the Texas Rangers' home ballpark in Arlington, Texas, would end even before that. It turns out they were hoping to help their borrower shortcut the path to the American dream. Instead they helped to create a financial crisis that they ultimately did not survive. At least that is what they were accused of.

As if the path to home ownership isn't intense already, the majority of potential homeowners, whether buying their first or fifteenth home, find choosing a real estate agent to represent them to be one of the most painful parts. Reports show that the top two or three traits buyers want in an agent are the exact same traits they find missing in many of their prior experiences. This does not have to be the case. Many of the nearly two million real estate agents in the United States of America are simply failing to deliver this dream in a desirable way because they're not committed, educated, capable, or working hard enough to come through for their home buyer clients.

There is, however, a small group of phenomenal real estate agents and brokers with a track record of success in all market conditions, systems for predictable results, and the resources and work ethic to deliver world-class value and expertise to home buyers. In doing so, they create confidence in their buyer clients and home ownership scenarios that bless clients for life.

REGS Publishing has assembled an amazing group of them to create the book you are now reading. They are not full-time authors, but the best of the best from the community of real estate agents. They each agreed to share actionable, helpful information that will serve nearly any home buyer in nearly any real estate market in America. From border to border, investments to luxury, and first homes to retirement properties, this select group of experts has shared insider tips to purchase, own, and enjoy the ideal property for you and/or your family.

Dive in and devour each chapter, underline and make notes in the margins, and then share this book or a key chapter with friends and family who could benefit. Resources like

FOREWORD

this are rare because gifted, successful, and generous men and women like this are rare. With 100 percent of book proceeds going to feed, shelter, educate, and serve children in need across the globe, these amazing professionals are not offering their hard-earned wisdom here for another dollar. Their goal is to break through the confusion and complexity of home buying and to serve folks in their communities and across America as you take on the adventure of the American dream.

As a broker myself and a consultant and coach to a select group of top agents in the world, I assure you that the American dream is still alive and well. In any market, regardless of mortgage interest rates, economic or political conditions, material costs, labor availability, and even global pandemics, home ownership ought to be the goal. Although the journey to buying a home can be more difficult at times, it is, and has always been, one of the single greatest routes to wealth accumulation and stability in the home, family, and community.

If you find yourself investigating your approach to purchasing your next property and you are fortunate enough to live in a community with one of these experts, you'd be wise to contact their offices directly. If you are not quite that lucky, reach out to the writer of whichever chapters have served you and inquire about a professional in your area that they may be able to connect you with.

It is no surprise that many home buyers, after having less than ideal experiences with real estate agents in the past, choose to go about buying a house all by themselves. However, this doesn't have to be the case. You do not have to approach such a significant decision and life moment without expertise, guidance, and advocacy. A resource like this can serve as a true and legitimate shortcut to success.

Take this shortcut!

—TODD TRAMONTE
Real Estate Broker, Best-selling Author,
Radio Host, Team Leader

THE POWER OF CASH

WITH ANDREW SMITH

ANDREW SMITH got his first taste of sales when he was nine. The young, aspiring entrepreneur sold baseball and football cards to middle schoolers on their way home! Growing up around parents and family who are entrepreneurs, Andrew had long considered the idea of building a business of his own, specifically within the world of residential real estate. Andrew now serves as a Realtor and Buyer Specialist on the Todd Tramonte Home Selling Team in Dallas-Fort Worth. He also has a knack for systems and execution so he serves informally in operational roles on the team as well.

Andrew and his high school sweetheart Becca moved to DFW in 2013 shortly after their wedding. Their college years forced them to date long-distance for four years while Andrew attended Baylor University, graduating with a degree in marketing, and Becca attended Mississippi

College. While Andrew misses the happy and delicious Cajun culture of his hometown of Lafayette, Louisiana, he loves the diverse opportunities that living in Texas provides and the buzz of living in a big city. Their heavy involvement and investment in both Watermark and CityBridge Community Church has helped them to plant deep roots in DFW.

Andrew and Becca have three kids. Currently, Nora is five and soon entering kindergarten, Cole is two and a half flying around on his bike, and Owen will be arriving on the scene any moment now to steal the show. Andrew enjoys every second that he gets to spend playing with his fun and energetic giggle monsters.

In their free time, Andrew and Becca devote a huge amount of time to people they are passionate about: relationships with their neighbors, their church, and ministries like Young Life. Andrew also enjoys working out, playing basketball, watching sports, following the latest installment in the Marvel Cinematic Universe, and digging into books about leadership and continuous improvement.

www.dallashomerealty.com
andrew@toddtramonte.com
(337) 212-6514

THE POWER OF CASH

> *"There are three forms of wealth
> you should obsess about:
> relationships, cash reserves,
> and long-term thinking."*
> —Todd Tramonte

The more cash you bring to the negotiation table, the more power and choice you have when it comes to buying a home. The amount of cash you have in the bank will help you win the home you want. You can weather the storms of life and home ownership more easily. The more cash you bring means paying less interest in the long-term. Your cash and connections to cash (relationships) show you are more stable to banks and sellers.

A lot of people think paying in cash for a house is something they'll never be able to afford. A mortgage is what they expect and think they'll have every house they ever own. But cash is powerful. On the other side, some are terrified of borrowing, hyper-conservative because they're only open to paying cash. Neither is necessarily right or wrong, but I'm excited to share three key principles of the power of using cash.

Principle #1: Cash gives you negotiating power

Buyers coming with all-cash reign supreme over the competition. When you come with an all-cash offer, people are more attracted to your offer. Sellers like all-cash offers because they come with the least number of contingencies which allow a potential buyer to back out. All-cash offers do not usually have financing contingencies which means they do not require an appraisal at all.

When it comes to negotiation, not only does cash remove complexity from financing, it speeds up the process. The seller may need to free up equity to move on to another purchase. You can close on a cash deal faster because you don't have to wait on banks, underwriters, or appraisers. Nobody else is requiring oversight. Therefore, cash is quick and compelling. The timeline to close on a home is faster with cash (under two weeks) than using a mortgage (30 days usually).

If you have a home and you would like to move from the starter home into something bigger for your family, maybe you have that much cash and you don't know it. By rolling the equity from your first home into your next home, that equity acts as cash when it comes to closing.

Even if you come with half-cash to a transaction, which means you're mortgaging the other half of the price of the house, the bank and seller are going to look at you more favorably. When you have a "loan to value ratio" at least 40-50%, the lender will rarely require an appraisal, which means you can offer an appraisal waiver to the seller, because there won't be an appraisal. In a seller's market, where offers are often going well above the starting list price, an appraisal waiver is a compelling tool that you can use to make sellers more easily take your offer.

Loan to value (LTV) ratio example - If you're bringing $300,000 in cash from savings and the sale of your previous home, and the house you win is $750,000, your LTV ratio ($300,000 divided by $750,000) is 40%.

The reason is if somehow you couldn't afford the mortgage payments if some unexpected event comes up, the bank has little doubt that they will be able to get their investment back. In other words, the lender is certain they will be able to sell the house for at least $450,000 to recoup their money.

All-cash offers and ones with mortgages give the seller the exact same amount of money. Cash excites sellers, even though in reality they are going to end up with the sales price no matter what the source. Even so, there's real value in that feeling and energy that comes from cash.

Principle #2: Cash saves you money in the long-run

If you bring cash to a home buying process, you're going to pay a lot less over time. You'll also save the most amount of money in comparison to people paying with mortgages because you're not paying interest. The more cash you put down, the less you'll have to borrow. And if you're not spending your hard-earned money on interest, you can put it to work in other places.

That's the biggest difference over the course of the lifetime of a loan: when you pay more cash, you save tens (or even hundreds) of thousands of dollars from the cost of the house, spread out over 15 or 30 years most commonly. When you compare the totals of how much you pay in principal versus interest at the end of 30 years on a mortgage at a 4.5% rate with no extra payments, that cost is 45% interest and 55% principal!

Thinking long-term allows you to pay less and save more over time. See how much interest you pay over the course of a 30 year mortgage on this chart:

Total principal and interest paid on a 30-year mortgage at 4.5% interest		
Principal	Interest	Total paid
$150,000	$123,609	$273,609
$200,000	$164,814	$364,814
$250,000	$206,018	$456,018
$300,000	$247,218	$547,218
$350,000	$288,423	$638,423
$400,000	$329,627	$729,627
$450,000	$370,832	$820,832

With all-cash offers, there are also one time fees that you save. You save money if you don't need an appraisal, typically required by lenders. An origination fee is a closing expense you don't have, which usually costs 1% of the mortgage. Even if you're not paying with all-cash, the smaller your mortgage, the smaller the corresponding origination fee, so there's an advantage there to bringing more cash to the table.

Now there is another side of this coin. Some people might say their cash is more valuable when placed in other investments. It's not about cost savings for them. It's about investment growth. You have to compare the interest rate versus the return rate that you're hoping for. However, that's less certain. It's possible that your investments do not have a more favorable rate of return. But one absolute certainty is that if you pay cash and don't borrow, you're not going to pay interest.

Principle #3: Cash gives you choice and flexibility

To the extent of cash you have, you have freedom to make the best decisions for you. Cash can give you clarity of thought because you're not distracted by minor issues or potentially needing to carry two mortgages. A healthy emergency fund and savings allows you to weather the storms of life easily. It can allow you to act fast without having an approval period. It gives you the choice of a small down payment or a big down payment, or even no loan at all. You start to have the whole spectrum open to you.

Cash gives you choices around time. If you or a seller are in a hurry, you can move quickly. When you're interested in slowing the process, cash is still highly motivating to the seller. They may give you a more flexible timetable or unusual terms because of the attractiveness and security of that cash.

Do you want to stretch your cash to get more house? Even when taking out a mortgage, cash extends your buying power. If you're showing up with a minimum down payment, then you can afford a minimum house, which is fine, but the more cash you have, the more house you can buy.

Cash gives you leverage. The more cash you have, the more house you could qualify for with a bank. For example, if I've got $10,000 cash to put down towards a 5% down payment, I can buy a $200,000 house. But if you wanted a million-dollar home and put 5% down, that would be just $50,000 (as long as you're comfortable with that mortgage payment). Just a little more cash becomes a lot more powerful.

On a different note, if you are paying all-cash you will have flexibility to access properties that would not qualify for financing. In addition to having more options, you will also have less competition for homes that are available only to cash buyers.

For example, if there's a house with a foundation problem, a bank is not going to approve that loan. The same would apply to roof damage, a fire in the kitchen, major plumbing or electrical issues. These are all things an appraiser, lender, or underwriter would literally disqualify. The home will need too much work and it's a potential liability to the lender.

The seller may not be willing to do those repairs, or they may not be able to afford to do those repairs. Do you have cash? Then you will really have the ability to negotiate a discount for the distressed property because the seller will be extremely limited by the number of buyers that can purchase it. This gives cash buyers a big advantage and negotiating power. You'll typically get a better deal with far less competition.

By using cash, you can narrow or eliminate the bidding war, access properties that might be available below market value and still benefit from all the traditional benefits of cash. That's a beautiful thing.

Bonus: Keys to accessing cash

Cash is powerful, but if I don't have much, what am I supposed to do? Is there any way to go?

There are options out there: relationships and services can get you access to cash.

Friends and family are a great option in this scenario. It's worth pursuing some pretty creative solutions where you may go so far as to borrow from friends of friends and you create some sort of scenario where you partner with them to get into a home and then you buy them out of it with traditional financing later.

Ask your family and friends who are well-resourced or rich in relationships; ask if they might be interested in or connect you with someone who would like to make a profitable short-term loan with a clearly communicated borrowing agreement for a couple months.

Here's an example: Say "I can get you a quick return on money you have sitting in savings. Would you be willing to float me the cash to buy a house for 30-60 days? After you give me the money, I will buy a house for cash for $450,000 or so. After closing, I will take out a traditional mortgage, and I'll give you back the $450K plus an additional $7,000. That rate of return is 1.55% in about 60 days, or 10% annualized. You could not get a better rate on your savings account or even in the stock market in most entire years!"

If you can't find any friends like that and prefer to use a service, Homeward is one company that essentially does the same thing as the scenario above. Using your real estate agent, Homeward actually buys a home for you in their name, and then you pay them back plus rent and a convenience fee, if applicable, often rolled into the new mortgage.

In Homeward's "Buy with Cash" program, if you use Homeward Mortgage, you effectively pay 0%, because you receive a credit at closing for the 1.9% convenience fee of their current service in Texas.

With Homeward's "Buy Before You Sell" program, even if you have a home you need to sell to purchase the next one, Homeward will pay cash to buy a home for you, you can move in and rent the home from them. Then, you can sell your last house (now vacant) without dealing with showings! Using Homeward Mortgage, this program costs you 1.4% convenience fee plus rent per day currently in Texas.

What about the appraised value of the home in this scenario? Homeward will get a third party to do a desktop appraisal within the mandatory 6 day option period they require. If there's a gap between the sales price and the appraisal that you cannot afford, then you can still "opt out" during the option period and get the 2% earnest money deposit they require back. In that scenario, all you paid was the option fee and cost to inspect the home. If you have the cash to float the gap, then you're closing in 2-3 weeks!

The point is this: you can buy in the strongest of seller's markets even if you have a house to sell with the power of cash. There are other services out there like Homeward like EasyKnock, Flyhomes, and Ribbon. This access to cash gives you a huge advantage when you go from "no one will accept my offer" to presenting ethically as a strong & quick cash offer on a home, without leaving you homeless or in a pinch with two mortgages or two moves to make!

On the other hand, in a buyer's market, this business model of "buy before you sell" or "pay with cash" goes away. There's just no need in that kind of market where buyers already have pretty natural leverage. In a market where sellers have tremendous leverage, cash really can get you in the game.

Partnering with an agent who knows how to put the right game plan into practice for you can really give you an advantage and get you the home that fits the needs of your family.

OLD HOMES
FOR BETTER VALUE

with Brandon Wyatt

BRANDON WYATT has called DFW home for his whole life, spending the majority of it in the Richardson and Garland area. Before Brandon joined the team as a buyer specialist, he worked with the team to purchase his most recent home in Rowlett. When he saw the high level of care that the team showed to him and his family, he knew this is where he wanted to work.

Brandon diligently works to break the stereotype of what people think of when they hear someone is a Realtor. His goal is to provide an extremely high level of value and care to his clients before, during, and after their transaction, but further to build lifelong friendships where he can add value long beyond a purchase or sale.

Caring for others in a time of need is nothing new for Brandon and Sarah, his wife of 13 years. They are committed to fostering children and have fostered 25 children over nine years. They have a deep conviction that they can make a profound impact by showing these children what a healthy, loving family looks like, even if it gets a little chaotic sometimes. They also adopted three brothers: Seth, 16, Jacob, 15, and Noah, 13.

Brandon and Sarah enjoy spending their family time playing board games and sports. Brandon also coaches their sons' little league sports, and he plays slowpitch softball, pickleball, and golf.

dallashomerealty.com
brandon@toddtramonte.com
(972) 333-1748

OLD HOMES FOR BETTER VALUE

A great strategy for some buyers is to go after a pre-existing home and restore it, or purchase an already fully restored older home, because there are major benefits compared to buying newer construction.

A lot of home buyers think they want a newer home because they believe it will entail less maintenance, and that it will also be cleaner, in a nicer area, and more impressive to their friends, family, and neighbors. They also mistakenly assume it will have amenities they wouldn't otherwise get. Because of that, many home buyers actually overlook the very real benefits of purchasing older homes.

When I meet with buyers, they often tell me they want a home in a great neighborhood. They want certain amenities. They know they want more space and more land and they believe a new build is the only way they're going to get it. In reality, they can have the neighborhoods and amenities they want at a better value if they shift their mindset to include the possibility of restoring older homes.

I think the biggest reason for these misconceptions is based on location. Think about how cities were developed. Most places in America were built around ports, railroads, and central hubs. For instance, I live in Dallas which was developed around the downtown area. You can clearly see rings of development. It started with a really close downtown ring and then expanded farther out over the decades.

If you are commuting to work, do you want to be closer or farther away? Location choice makes a big difference, because I see buyers overpaying to get into neighborhoods that really don't fit their larger priorities.

Think about what you find most valuable. Is it your commute? Hobbies? Maybe your church? Where do you like to spend free time? And what do you like to spend time doing? Let these considerations weigh into your approach to deciding on location.

With this in mind, you will find that new homes are not necessarily in the best location. They're almost always farther away from the downtown area, because that's where the land was available to develop. On the off chance that you find a new home in a centralized location the price will likely be much higher because it was built on the last plot of land available. It's difficult to get the best value by buying the newest homes in that area.

A recent report from the Texas Real Estate Research Center showed that newer homes sell for 14% more than existing homes in the Dallas/Fort Worth area. That means a home that sells for $360k would cost you $410k to build.

Another big benefit of considering older homes is that every house will have similar issues. Mother Nature doesn't care how old your home is. If it hails or a tornado whips through town, the property is going to be affected the same way as the one next to it. There will be no difference between older construction versus newer. They'll both take the same damage.

There are four aspects of a home that experience wear and tear though that you should consider. The "Big Four" include: electrical, plumbing, foundation, and roof.

As we're doing an inspection of a house, if the roof is 20 years old in Texas, that's about the end of its life cycle. In other parts of the country, it could be a little bit longer or possibly a bit shorter. Most will wear out between that 10-20 year mark.

This means that buying a house that is 25 years old will likely give you much greater value because a majority of issues will have been repaired. You'll essentially be buying a new home in an older location because the roof and water heater and A/C will have been replaced and the foundation has already settled. Since most foundations come with a lifetime warranty, these things add up to extreme value. You definitely don't want to buy a house and then turn around in a year and spend another $10-20k for a new air-conditioning unit when that could be avoided.

Oftentimes buyers are thinking or feeling one way about the home purchase, but later regret not considering the larger picture. Maybe they have seen amenities at someone else's home, or on a television show, and they think the only way to get that is from a new build. They can become so concerned with the big kitchen that they overlook small bedrooms.

Right now in most markets, new homes are taking quite a long time to be built. Recently one closed almost a year after we signed the contract. The builder kept pushing back the timeline. Now, imagine how you would feel if you expected to move in during early summer when you'd planned to take time off. But now it's November and it's cold and miserable. And you're stuck on the builder's schedule.

Alternatively, if you're open to buying an older home, you can go in and fix it the way you want in any season or time of year. It can all be on your schedule. Do you want new floors? You can put in new flooring. New cabinetry? You can have new cabinetry installed. If you sign a contract for such services in June, they're most likely going to be installed in June, July, or maybe August, because these renovations take less time.

What are your time and energy worth? Like most of us Americans, we live in a "microwave generation." If I put something in the microwave, I want it now. When it comes to homes, I put down my money for flooring because I want that now. I place a deposit for painting that I want done now.

When we talk about landscaping, many buyers want a home with established trees, or privacy bushes. What they don't realize is that having trees either takes time or a lot of money.

During the time you spend waiting for a new build, the misconception is that once you get into the home, everything is going to be perfect. Well... there's no such thing as a perfect new home. That's why builders offer a warranty. In a year, if something has happened, they will come in and replace it. But are you prepared to wait that year?

When it comes to buying an older home, if warranties are something that help you sleep better at night, then you can purchase a home warranty from a reputable company to help defray the cost of any potential repairs.

Also bear in mind, that "older" doesn't necessarily have to imply *old*. Any pre-existing home will offer many of the same benefits when compared to purchasing new construction. Even if you don't care about charm and character and age, the value of buying a two-year-old home might be better than buying new construction, simply because someone else worked out all the kinks in those first couple of years.

It's funny how many people will build a brand new home and try to make it look old on purpose. There is a huge trend for hand-scraped hardwood floors. Many want to fill their new homes with antique furniture. They'll even buy Edison light bulbs, attempting to make new technology look old. If that's something you enjoy, you should definitely consider purchasing an older property instead.

Again, "old" doesn't have to mean 100 years old. It might mean 40, 50, or 60 years old. Either way, you'll be able to enjoy the look and feel and cost savings by not remaining glued to the idea of buying new construction.

A client told me they were moving for their job, but when I asked them questions, I discovered the real reason for the move was that they wanted to spend more time with friends. It was important to them to have a shorter commute, so buying new construction was restrictive. We talked about the possibilities of an older home that would be just a five-minute drive to work. This idea really gelled because now the gentleman is home every day for lunch, and every night for dinner with his kids and family. Buying a pre-existing home turned out to be the ideal situation.

The same couple decided to repaint everything and make upgrades throughout including replacement windows, but when I ran the numbers for them, they still saved almost $50,000 over buying new construction. Even so, the benefits of having more time to spend as a family was the ultimate reward.

Another friend was interested in more land, but didn't want to move so far from schools, church, friends, job and recreation. In order to do that, they purchased a much older home that was not in great shape, but was located on a couple of acres in the exact location they wanted. They were able to completely renovate that home and revitalize the lot. With fresh landscaping and lighting, they added a pool and basketball court, a pond and even a fruit orchard, garden and greenhouse. This large property gave them so many options, they were able to do everything they ever dreamed of on a lower budget and much quicker... for probably half of what it would've cost to buy a new home. The truth is there wasn't even anything available of that size and scope in new construction if they'd been tied to the idea of only buying new.

There's nothing wrong with a new house, but the problem is that quite a few buyers don't even consider an older home when there are so many benefits. Just remember to consider the possibilities of purchasing a pre-existing home. After evaluating both options, you can decide whether location is more attractive than having brand new heating and air-conditioning systems. Perhaps the list price of an older home will allow room in your budget to replace the roof, update the windows, or install new plumbing, electrical, doors, or even countertops. In that case, it's the best of both worlds. You save money while finding the charm and character you were looking for. Plus you can get into that home far more quickly.

Think about your parents' or grandparents' house, and all the memories you have from that home. Was it new construction? Or was that an older home?

What are your fondest memories growing up? Maybe it was in a brand new home with spotless marble, but maybe it was the smell of the wood in your grandparents' house where you played hide and seek, or the cabinet where the candy was stored, or the bunk bed that you and your cousin shared at the holidays.

Remember that a house is just a house, but a home is what you make it.

FINDING A HOUSE FOR RETIREMENT

WITH DINO DINENNA

DINO DiNENNA has been a Hilton Head Island and Bluffton, South Carolina, local since 1993, about a month after his first visit. He originally hails from the Washington Metropolitan area, where he began selling real estate in the Northern Virginia and Maryland markets in 1987 at the age of eighteen. Within months, while majoring in Business with a concentration in Real Estate & Urban Development at George Mason University, he became a top producer in his office and hasn't stopped since.

Involved in many aspects of the real estate industry from residential and commercial sales to spec rehab and development of homes, Dino specializes in luxury and investment real estate. He is recognized among the top 3% of agents nationwide as a Certified Residential Specialist, a Certified Negotiation Expert, and has served on the Hilton Head Area Association of Realtors® Board of Directors as well as its Professional Development Committee.

A believer in experiential education and adventurous exploration, he's traveled through many parts of the world, having lived seasonally in Italy and Hawaii. Locally, you'll often see Dino sharing the beauty and wonder of the Lowcountry with his wife Ashley and their daughter Alessandra.

hiltonheadrealtysales.com
dino@hiltonheadrealtysales.com
(843) 560-9310

FINDING A HOUSE FOR RETIREMENT

What lifestyle do you want to live?

Are you planning to be active in retirement? Do you want to be in a place with lots of open space and outdoor activities? Or do you prefer somewhere closer to a city with all the arts and restaurants and the late-night stuff that goes on there?

Do you want to live in a community that includes amenities, or where *a la carte* options like club memberships and golf packages are offered? Deciding on the right type of community for your goals makes selecting the home much simpler.

First, envision your lifestyle day to day, week to week, month to month. What does that look like? Once you have this identified, we can determine a property that will help make your goals happen.

Some mistakes people make when trying to make this decision include buying based on a magazine vision, or simply copying what their friends have done.

What's the best approach? Usually there's a split. You have half who are methodical and do understand their long-term vision. Others say, "Hey, I'm going to buy based on the cheapest price and size," and they focus on the house first and not the community. But while they're thinking that they can get a house for a certain amount of money, they neglect to think about where it is located in relation to everything they want to do. Consequently, they spend a lot of time not enjoying where they live, and then wind up selling that property and buying another to get the lifestyle they truly want.

When you get clear on the lifestyle you want to live, you'll be able to find the right property, the right location, the right size, and maintain the right budget.

This may point you toward a 55+ community, with a vibe that offers activity options and amenities geared toward a similar age group. Or it may point you toward a Country Club community that offers the whole lifestyle, but without the retirement community feel—more of a club mentality. Residents do many things like golfing and boating together, and even parties.

A middle ground would be finding a traditional home, with social clubs or activity hubs easily accessible, but not required. Some of these listings are in areas of investor properties, bringing a constant parade of Airbnb or VRBO traffic to the neighborhood. This would be a great fit for someone who loves meeting new people because the activity and hustle-bustle will allow you to still feel in the thick of it. "I may be retiring, but I'm not old." But if you aren't interested in that atmosphere, being surrounded by short-term rental properties can create a nightmare environment.

How can you go about getting more clarity on which of those communities is best for you? Are there resources? Do you need a real estate agent to help? Do you need someone on the ground in the location where you're aspiring to be, or can you handle everything online?

You can find a lot of factual information on the internet, but until you set foot in a community, you won't have a feel for what you're looking at. When buying from afar, it's critical to have someone who can guide you. Many communities are gated and you won't have access to them without the help of an agent. Until you can set foot behind the gates of many of the communities, you'll have little to no idea of the different vibe in each community.

We've had a few clients who insisted the house they saw advertised was the one for them, but after they visited, they realized there was no way they could tolerate the neighborhood. That's a big waste when flying across the country. In black and white terms, it's easy to suggest a certain number of bedrooms and bathrooms, even square footage, but something like ease of access due to traffic or tourists, or proximity to amenities can be tricky to determine when you don't live there. It may look like it's only two-tenths of a mile from the beach or golf course, but in traffic the time is excruciating.

Some people believe it's possible to select a house based on price per square foot. In that case they usually end up with a house they don't want. Why? Because you can pack a house with square footage that's not usable. We had one client who bought a 4,600 square feet house... but the hallways were six feet wide. Every stairway landing was the size of a small room. That chewed up valuable living space. Especially in retirement, consider how much you want to clean. How much square footage do you want to heat? How much do you want to cool?

Taking the next step

Once you've decided what you want, how do you go about securing that property? You may need to sell your current home. Buying a new house is difficult enough in the same town, but in two different geographical locations, you've got more to coordinate. To compound the problems, many areas will not accept a contract contingent on you selling your current home.

You will have to figure out how to best get out of one home and into another. If your previous house is paid for, that's a lot easier, but if you're covering two mortgage payments, you don't want to risk your financial security. It will be important to explore financing options in the area where you are looking to buy. If you're not paying cash, you need a lender who is familiar with the area and its idiosyncrasies.

Again, it's helpful to have a local advocate. In some cases, we have been able to alert clients to issues they would not otherwise have known. "Hey, I know we fell in love with that house, but there were fifteen minutes worth of cars waiting to make that right turn at the next big block."

These kinds of issues won't change for three or four years because builders are adding homes quickly. None of that information is on the internet. You need a real estate agent who is willing to research all the details for you and have your best interests at heart.

I'm biased as a great real estate agent with a team who will do that for you, but not all agents are equal. You're going to have to be careful to find someone who truly does know the specific property type and part of town and lifestyle you want to live and can help lead, guide and counsel you through that.

I had one client who had been vacationing in my area for years and years. When they decided to retire here, I took them on tours of the six different gated communities that matched their criteria. We spent time exploring until they were able to narrow it down to the one community they wanted plus another they would consider. Then we focused on getting the house they wanted in that community. Nine years later, they're still loving both the house and the community.

There's also the gradual approach where you rent or purchase something in the area you're interested in, before you retire, so you can begin to enjoy the lifestyle and learn more about the communities and amenities available in the vicinity. Once you make an initial investment in a property, you can get to know the community by visiting a few times each year. You can get to know what life is like in different seasons, whether that's winter versus summer or off-season versus tourist season. Then you can sell that property and roll into another, more ideal long-term home. Or possibly you could hold that first property as an investment and add additional cashflow to your retirement through short-term rentals.

As humans, we value property differently in retirement. People in their thirties and forties often focus on proximity to work or the needs of their children. Retirement is different. You finally get to choose a house based on the life *you want to live*. It may not be quantifiable in bedrooms, bathrooms, square footage, or lot size. A lifestyle offers a different value system. The math may be more or less important when it comes to comparable pricing. If I'm 63 and I've got the money, I'm less concerned with bargain hunting. If it feels right for you, especially if this is the last house you want to live in, then you should enjoy it every day like a vacation.

You want this house to be a home run. It isn't about where the kids drop their books after school. You want to be comfortable, living the life of your dreams, not just with selfish comforts, but also having purpose and meaning.

As you approach retirement, make it a priority to meet with a knowledgeable agent. Spend time chatting with them from afar and in person. Help them understand what you're looking for in your retirement home. Then and only then can they truly help you fulfill those dreams and secure the lifestyle you want for your best years to come.

WRITING AN OFFER TO GET THE HOUSE YOU REALLY WANT

WITH JOELLE DOWE

JOELLE DOWE is a native Texan and a 20+ year Austinite. After many years of being a top-producing software sales executive and leader in Austin's booming tech industry, Joelle pivoted her deal-making skills to her true passion of real estate.

Match-making people with properties is what makes Joelle's heart sing. She is both passionate and highly proficient at being in tune with her clients' needs to successfully navigate a real estate transaction. Joelle uses her breadth and depth of the latest technology trends to help serve her clients all the while handling the buying and selling of properties with the utmost efficiency and expertise.

On a personal level, Joelle is married to coffee-junkie Dan and also has two wonderful sons. Joelle enjoys traveling, tacos, fitness, and spending time with friends. Joelle is currently on the hunt for the best Taco in Austin.

www.letsmoveaustin.com
joelle@letsmoveaustin.com
(512) 826-7106

WRITING AN OFFER TO GET THE HOUSE YOU REALLY WANT

Congratulations! You know you want to buy a home and you have the cash or financing locked and loaded. Now what? What will you need to know in order to secure your dream house?

Before you do anything more, you need a keen understanding of local market conditions. You may have a general idea from watching the news, but a true professional in the industry will understand what it takes for your offer to have the best chance of winning in real-time.

Where I live and work in Austin, Texas, we are experiencing unprecedented market conditions. Tech giants such as Oracle and Tesla have relocated their headquarters here. Samsung is also setting up huge operations in our area as well as many other employers both large and small. In short, Austin currently is a unicorn for growth and there are simply not enough homes being built to satisfy the demand. An unrepresented buyer striking out on their own to purchase in such unbalanced conditions doesn't really have a fighting chance.

A comical way of thinking of this market is like a game of Musical Chairs:

> # The Musical Chairs of Real Estate
>
> ## Buyer's Market
>
> In a buyer's market,
> you have **8 chairs** and
> only **5 people** are playing.
>
> ## Seller's Market
>
> In a seller's market,
> you have **5 chairs** and
> **8 people** are playing.
>
> ## Today's Market
>
> In today's market,
> you have **2 chairs**,
> **123 players**,
> and **1 chair** just got sold.

Although the vignette is satire, it is all too real for buyers trying to land a home.

A seller's market is completely different from a buyer's market, and both are unique compared to a balanced or more stable market. The pacing required is also completely different, as is the structure of successful offers.

A seller's market means there are more people looking to buy than there are homes available. In that type of market, buyers have less negotiating power.

In a buyer's market, by contrast, there are more homes for sale than there are buyers. Buyers can expect to have more negotiating power.

In stable markets, there is a balance between buyers and sellers, and the negotiation power between the parties is more even.

Let's take a closer look at how we define these different types of markets.

A general rule of thumb is this:

Seller's Market: 0-4 Months of Inventory

Balanced Market: 5-7 Months of Inventory

Buyer's Market: 8+ Months of Inventory

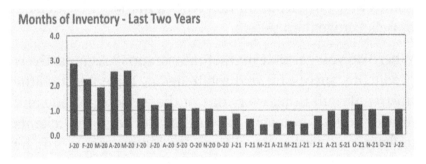

The Months of Inventory Chart[1] above represents the actual inventory listed on the Austin Multiple Listing Service (MLS) in 2020-2022. In Austin, it was a seller's market these last two years, with less than 3 months of

---

[1] Based on information from the Austin Board of REALTORS® (alternatively, from ACTRIS). Neither the Board nor ACTRIS guarantees or is in any way responsible for its accuracy. The Austin Board of REALTORS®, ACTRIS and their affiliates provide the MLS and all content therein "AS IS"' and without any warranty, express or implied. Data maintained by the Board or ACTRIS may not reflect all real estate activity in the market.

inventory each month during this time period. "Months' supply" refers to the number of months it would take for the current inventory of homes on the market to sell out completely given the current sales pace.

A seller's market is when buyers have less than four months of inventory available to choose from. When there are not a lot of homes for buyers to choose from, buyers have to compete to get the best home. Sellers have most, if not all, of the leverage in this type of market.

Four to seven months of housing inventory means an area won't run out of houses for four to seven months even if no new homes enter the market. A buyer's market is when we have more than seven months' worth of inventory, meaning it takes a while to get a home sold, so buyers have a lot of homes to choose from. In this type of market, buyers have more leverage than sellers.

Where do you get that market information? As an actively producing, successful real estate agent, I live and breathe this reality full time, every day of the week. I provide and utilize vetted industry resources to help my clients understand current conditions by boiling down all the overwhelming complexities of that data. You can turn to us to provide the data, parse it, and put it into a format that's really easy to use.

Some people call this housing inventory number the "absorption rate." Simply put, the absorption rate is a measure of supply and demand. If we have 3.6 months' worth of inventory, the absorption rate is 3.6, because that is how fast we're buying the homes that are available. It's a lot like a stock ticker where you get a quick snapshot of where any stock is at that point in time. You learn the Dow Jones industrial average is up 100 points today, or the

NASDAQ is down 1.5%. Those are quick numbers people use to get a read on the market as a whole. The absorption rate is the best number to look at to get your read on the whole residential market in any one city, zip code, state, or county.

Absorption rates can vary within cities. The broader the geographic area you are looking at, the less accurate the numbers become because they are so diluted with data. For example, a hot central neighborhood like Travis Heights could be a seller's market while a neighborhood on the outskirts of Austin—like Manor or Kyle where builders are flooding the market with inventory—could be a buyer's market. Both are close to Austin but have different absorption rates based on location and available inventory.

Seller's market

Here's what I explain to my buyer clients in our initial consultation. If you know for a fact that you are in a seller's market, you will want to focus your offer on whatever is important to the seller. Meet all of those requests that you possibly can.

You do need to think about your budget though. Know the amount you are comfortable paying, whether it's cash or using a loan amount. Set a boundary up front because a seller's market is going to pressure you to spend all of your budget. You must set your personal line at a number you really can live with. That's not "how much you can spend," according to a financier, but instead it's "how much you would spend before you go crazy and your house becomes a burden instead of a joy."

In a seller's market you also need to be prepared to work fast. Sellers have all the leverage. You may not be able to get the first house you place an offer on.

Specific things to help your offer win in a seller's market

Have a pre-approval letter for your financing

A pre-approval letter is different from a PreQualification (PQ) letter. A PQ is not as thorough and just means that the mortgage lender has reviewed the financial information you have provided and believes you will qualify for a loan. A pre-approval letter holds more weight when attached to an offer because it shows the listing agent that you have taken the steps necessary to verify that you are qualified for a loan and have provided proof. It is the next step beyond a PQ in the loan approval process and is a conditional commitment from the lender to loan you the money for a mortgage.

Waive appraisal

An appraisal waiver means you would waive the right to renegotiate if the lender's appraisal comes in lower than the purchase price. This gives the seller more security by knowing you will cover the cost difference if this happens and are less likely to terminate the contract and not close.

Set a short inspection period

This gives the seller more security by limiting the number of days you ask for in order to perform inspections.

Place high earnest money

Earnest money is funds put down on a house to show the seller you are serious about closing. This money is also known as a "good faith deposit." This is money the seller will keep if you back out of the contract. It compensates them for the time their home is off the market.

Pay everything you possibly can

For example, you might pick up the cost of a title policy or new survey, if needed.

Offer to pay HOA transfer fees

These are generally in the $200-500 range.

Offer free seller leaseback

If seller leaseback is important to the seller, put that front and center. Offering this option shows that you are flexible and are willing to work within their moving timeframe.

Offer an incentive

This is where you can get creative. I've seen everything ranging from luxury cruises to lawn care for a year.

Things normally done in contract negotiation that YOU SHOULD NOT DO in a seller's market

In a seller's market, you will want to make sure you do not do anything that will make the seller go out of their way to accommodate your offer.

Don't ask for a seller credit

A seller credit is money the seller must give the buyer at closing as an incentive to purchase a property.

Don't ask the seller to purchase a home warranty

If a home warranty is important to you, then make sure you are prepared to cover its cost yourself.

Don't ask for anything that will cost the seller additional money

In a seller's market, your offer will likely face stiff competition. When you ask for items that will have a financial impact on the seller, it weakens your offer.

Don't ask for things that make your offer inconvenient for the seller

You want your offer to be competitive in every way. When you ask for items that will hold back the seller from realizing their own financial and housing dreams, you decrease the likelihood that your offer will be accepted.

Buyer's market

In a buyer's market, homes are plentiful and there are choices galore. It's easy to get overwhelmed by the amount of homes available. The sense of urgency to buy may be lax because of the sheer quantity available and because the competition isn't there.

When I work with clients, we discuss their must-haves and stick to those. Otherwise you will find yourself searching for way too long and holding out for the perfect house (which usually doesn't exist). In most cases, it's rare for someone to not have even one thing they'd change about a house. Even those who have built multimillion-dollar custom homes list choices they would have made differently. Creating realistic expectations and sticking to your must-haves will save both your sanity and time in the long run.

After searching for their perfect house with no luck, John and Christina bought land in a gated community and built their custom dream home. Although the house was built to their exact specifications, a year later Christina still had things she wished she had done differently. She wished she'd had the architect design the windows closer to the floor. So, it goes to show that even if you have the house custom built from scratch, there inevitably will be something you would have changed or done differently. The best thing to do is to pick the best house that has your must-haves and don't look back.

The structure of your offer in this market is the opposite of the seller's market and you are more likely to get the seller to contribute financially toward your bottom line.

Stable market

The massive benefit to a buyer in a stable market is that, generally speaking, sellers are aware that they're going to have to give a little to get a little, and buyers are typically aware that they're going to have to give a little to get a little. This creates a much higher spirit of cooperation.

Most real estate agents also know that in this type of market, a home can sit a little bit longer, but not terribly long. Things don't happen overnight, but they don't take forever either. A buyer can typically get the primary things they want, but not every single thing. Also, sellers can usually get the key things they want, but not every dream or desire.

If a buyer passes, the seller can be confident they'll find another buyer. If a buyer passes on one home, they can be confident they'll find another house. This is a market where buyers can usually sleep on a decision for one night and also have enough options to be really, really happy with the final house they choose. This is a market that's much more even keeled, more comfortable, and honestly, more fun.

Timing is everything depending on the market you're in.

Sellers could be coming into this thinking, *It's probably going to take me 100-180 days to sell.* The buyer doesn't have to panic. They can visit an open house and not worry it might be sold that night. But be aware that it could sell any day now.

When I advise buyers who are house hunting in a buyer's market, I explain that, if you see a house and it had four other showings that day, then treat that more like a seller's market approach, but nowhere near as extreme. You might need to drop a few of those little nuggets that will be really attractive to the seller... offering to pay title, nice earnest money. You don't have to be over the top, but you can select a few items that are most comfortable for you to help your contract offer stand out.

If you offered that in a stable market, that would not be necessary. But if you offer to pay title or give them a free leaseback, that's going to jump out because that's totally uncommon in this market.

Some options include offering higher earnest money, a shorter option period, higher option fee offering to pay seller's fees. Now in this market, you can ask for the seller to pay some of those fees. If there is not a tremendous amount of competition, you can get the seller to pay the title insurance policy.

You do have a really good shot of the seller providing a survey or getting you one if it's needed. You've got about a 50/50 shot at getting the seller to provide a home warranty or some product warranties. You've also got a balanced opportunity to get the seller to leave some appliances, furniture, or non-realty items.

You can include these things into the offer. Your overall message in the stable market is that an individual house could still be more or less competitive. So now you need to feel it out, preferably by having an agent reach out to the seller or the seller's agent to get to know their situation, their timeline, their motivation and need, because it could be leaning toward a buyer market or seller market.

In a stable market you've got to be much more attentive, but you don't have to be as urgent. Ask the seller or their agent whether this house feels like it's leaning a little seller-side or a little buyer-side. If it's the most beautiful house in the neighborhood and it's priced well, it's almost always going to lean toward the seller's advantage. On the other hand, if a house has good bones, but doesn't look great, it's going to lean towards the buyer's market. This gives the buyer a little power there because the sellers aren't set up for maximum success.

Over 20 years ago, when my husband and I bought our first home in Austin, it was a buyer's market and the area where we bought was in a new subdivision in the southwest part of town. The house we made an offer on was two years old and the husband had just been promoted in a job transfer out of town. There were new homes being built on the street and ours had been sitting on the market for 93 days. People looking to buy in the neighborhood wanted the new homes that had never been lived in which is why the house we were looking at had been languishing for over 3 months. We were able to negotiate a reduction in list price and the seller's employer even paid money toward our closing costs.

If you have the right agent on your team, even when the situation might seem bleak, there's a silver lining. One of my clients was a couple who took a longer time to make a decision because they were out-of-state buyers who came to visit a home three times. Because of delayed decision-making, we missed the house. It was under contract before my buyers decided to submit an offer, but I called the listing agent and asked if they had any backup offers. They did not and we submitted a backup offer right away. Five days later when the earlier contract fell through escrow, our offer moved into first place and my clients won the house.

We covered a lot of technical aspects of contract possibilities, but remember it almost always comes down to more than just the technical details. It helps to have someone on your team who can bring that all together for you. Often the best real estate agents have built solid relationships with other agents in their market and can give you an inside track on finding out what is important to the seller so you can benefit most.

When you have the right approach, or the right agent who has the right approach, you can be confident in winning in any market.

BUYING & SELLING SIMULTANEOUSLY

WITH JOHN BYERS

JOHN BYERS has been in real estate since 2002. After graduating from Texas A&M University, he took a Commission with the United States Air Force, attaining the rank of Captain. He later moved to Houston, TX, where he began working for State Farm Insurance. State Farm relocated him to the College Station/Bryan area and into a technology training position.

After ten years in the corporate world, John decided to pursue a career in real estate. He has co-owned three national real estate franchises and now owns one of the fastest growing independent brokerages in College Station, TX.

He is married to Cindy, and they have two beautiful daughters, Elizabeth and Rebekah. John enjoys leading in his church's Singles Ministry and traveling with his family.

Their goal is to visit all 50 states before the girls graduate college. When not working in real estate or traveling, you will find John at home working on his farm just outside College Station.

www.towerpointteam.com
john@towerpointteam.com
(979) 412-1601

BUYING & SELLING SIMULTANEOUSLY

When buying and selling at the same time what do you fear? Most people will answer, *"The unknown!"*

Have you ever watched a Scooby-Doo cartoon? They are some of my family's favorites. Even though Shaggy and Scooby know it's safer to stick with the gang, they always get separated from their team and get into a frightful mess. They also stumble into the solution and solve the mystery... however, that only happens in a cartoon. To solve the mystery of buying and selling at the same time, you need to stay with the team!

Buying and selling a home at the same time presents several challenges. The goal of this chapter is to help you understand how to plan for and navigate each of those hurdles.

Most of my clients want to identify a new home, get it under contract, sell the existing home, avoid two mortgages, and only move once—thus avoiding "The Homeless Gap."

Before we jump into the mechanics of buying and selling at the same time, let's understand a few of the terms associated with buying and selling.

What is a Buyer's Market?

A buyer's market occurs when there are more homes available than there are buyers looking for homes. In a buyer's market it is easier to find a new home than to sell your old one. Sellers are often willing to accept contingent offers in a buyer's market.

What is a Seller's Market?

A seller's market is the opposite of a buyer's market. It is a market in which there are more buyers than sellers. In a seller's market it is highly likely your old home will sell more quickly than you will be able to find and buy a new home. In a seller's market it is not as likely that a contingent offer will be considered.

What is a Contingent Offer?

A Contingent Offer occurs when a deal is dependent on something else before the purchase can be completed. A common contingency is the sale of another property before the purchase of the new property. In this situation the seller agrees to sell you his home but knows that the sale of his home is "contingent" or dependent upon you selling your old home first. Another common contingency is a mortgage. Purchasing the home with a mortgage makes the purchase contingent on two things—the buyer being qualified to secure a loan to buy the house, and the house meeting the requirements set by the lender. There are other contingencies but these two are well known.

What does "Real Estate Professional" mean?

Most states have qualifications to obtain a real estate agent license. To be a professional realtor means that you have relevant experience, continually seek out current industry best practices, are an expert in your market, and provide services in a consistent world-class manner. Most agents do not have the systems or experience, nor do they consistently work to improve those systems beyond practicing on real clients. Finding a real estate professional may require several interviews, seeking referrals from someone who has used the professional in the past, or reading reviews of past clients' experiences.

What is meant by "financial situation"?

Knowing your financial situation means that you have a clear understanding of the cash reserves required for closing costs to buy and sell, the amount of liquid funds you have on hand, your credit score and ability to get financing if needed, as well as other resources like a gift from a relative or investments for retirement.

NOTE: Before utilizing investments designated for retirement, it is wise to check with a financial planner or CPA to understand if there are any tax consequences from accessing those funds before relying upon them.

How to buy and sell simultaneously while avoiding the homeless GAP!

Your timeline will be critical to accomplishing this. Most people who want to buy and sell at the same time have one fear... becoming homeless between the time they have sold their old house and the time they can move into their new home. This is called "The Gap."

Let's examine the ways you can avoid The Gap or at the very least manage it, especially with the help of a real estate professional.

Step One
Just like presidents give a State of the Union Address and governors give a State of the State address, you need to know the state of your local market. Is it a buyer's market, or is it a seller's market, or something in between?

Whether you are in a buyer's market or a seller's market, there are always homes that seem not to sell. At the time of writing, it is an extreme seller's market in my area, with only 145 single family homes available. Average days on market is around 30—an historic low—and closings are happening in far less than the normal 115 days. Of the 145 active homes on the market, 47 have been there well over 45 days, some over 90 days.

Knowing your market means knowing what it is about homes the market has rejected and why they are not selling. If you want to successfully buy and sell at the same time, you need to make certain your existing home will not fall victim to the same thing that is keeping those "Dead 45" on the market, unable to attract buyers.

There are many reasons the market may reject a home. When working with a professional realtor, they will be willing to give an honest and thorough evaluation of your existing home and how to best position it to sell within your timeline.

Step Two
Next is to evaluate the "State of Your Affairs." This includes the state of your finances, needs, wants, and dreams. Your personal situation really does make a difference, especially if there is another decision maker involved like a spouse.

Back before I was in real estate and newly married, my wife asked me, "So, what do you want in a home?" I shared with her that I wanted about fifty acres, somewhere we could build close enough to town but have a buffer between us and the neighbors. I excitedly "dreamt aloud" for 15-20 minutes until we were close to home. I noticed she had become quiet, but didn't think to ask about what she was thinking about until the next day. She began to animatedly share with me concerns, anxiety, and worry that flooded over her because we were in no financial position to buy fifty acres, much less manage it and move that far out of town! She enjoyed being in town, close to work, close to shopping, and close to family! What was I thinking?!

What I had not realized was that my dreaming out loud caused an overwhelming amount of fear and frustration for her. I quickly explained that I was just dreaming. Part of knowing your situation, your "State of Personal Affairs," is knowing what you *both* want, when you want it, and what you are prepared to buy and when... especially if there are other decision-makers who need to be involved.

Now is the time to sit down and visit with each stakeholder about these kinds of issues. It will help you be prepared in Step 4 to find exactly what you want to buy. Now twenty years later, my wife has not divorced me, and we have found the perfect eight acres just outside of town on which we built a house we both designed.

Be prepared to work through and discuss with all decision-makers (and your real estate professional) what you expect to happen during the process. Just bear in mind that if you have an extensive list of absolute, must-have features for the home, your list of potential properties will be reduced greatly.

My clients Seth and Aimee currently have a home they love but would like it to have more space around them. They have a large family and know they must have at least five bedrooms with at least three bathrooms. They know they want it on at least one and a half or more acres of land and it must be within 15 minutes (maybe 20) out of town. In a buyer's market this might be easy, but we are currently in a seller's market, and they understand it may take a long while to find.

In this step you want to work to understand the current market and how your choices affect the available houses to view. Knowing this will keep you from wasting time looking at houses you will not buy, or from buying a house you will not want. You need to build in a certain level of flexibility. Regardless of the market, issues can creep up that are unexpected and unforeseeable. Also sitting down with a Professional Realtor will help you realize some of the issues that will pop up in any transaction.

Step Three

The third step is getting your home ready to sell, which comes before looking to see what you want to buy, regardless of market temperature. At the John Byers team we have 7 strategies to sell your home for over-the-average price in under-the-average time which are essential for maximizing your profit.[2]

First, let's talk about inspections. Pre-inspection of your home before you put it on the market will save you time, frustration, and quite likely money. You will be able to control the information and eliminate deal killers long before you even list your home.

Another part of our strategy is staging. Staging has become an extremely popular word however, but we don't mean interior design. Staging is the positioning items in your home's living space to help any potential buyer see the space in a more favorable light. Photography, specifically, professional photography is vital. Regardless of the market,

---

[2] We cover many of these strategies in *The Ultimate Guide to Selling Your Home*, REGS, 2021.

professional photography makes a dramatic difference. Our first showing is online. Photography has been called our most important technology!

Next we need to talk about marketing. There are several types of marketing that come into play. The first is targeting broad groups of people, hitting the largest potential market of buyers possible. The other and even more potent marketing is identifying the likely buyer then fine-tuning the marketing message to that group. Don't avoid what makes your home unique, identify it. Make your house a unique market of One.

Our systematic approach allows you to focus on the details that come with a move while we focus on selling and then eventually helping you buy. Once you are prepared to sell, you can then focus on becoming prepared to buy. If the temperature of the market is a hot seller's market, waiting until the optimum time to go active will help with closing the gap between the buy and the sale. If the market is cooler for sales, getting to market sooner may be the best option.

If you are selling in a seller's market that may work out to your benefit as you sell. Sellers are often able to get buyers to agree to delay their move-in after closing for a period of time. That time can be used to locate, negotiate, and close on the new house. The more upfront searching you do the more likely you are to have a new house in mind. In a seller's market the more preparation you have put into the existing home to have it ready to sell, the better off you will be.

Once the staging is done, the professional photography is proofed, and you identify the home you want, your existing house can go live on the market. The instant or just before you are under contract on the new house your existing home must go live.

As a buyer there are usually a couple of ways out of a deal, as a seller you are not obligated to sell your house until you actually sign the contract. That means you have a window of opportunity to coordinate all the details on both sides. If you close on the sale of your existing home a day or two before you buy the new home, the dollars from the sale will be available to use to buy the new house. With a leaseback in place on your old home, you will then have time to pack, load, and move into the new house without a gap, avoiding homelessness.

Jim and Ginger had been building their new home for several months. As it neared completion, they decided it was time to turn on the marketing for their existing home. The inspections had been done, repairs were complete, photography had been taken, and marketing materials had been created. All that remained was to turn on the marketing. In a matter of days, they received an offer that was surprising even to them! We countered back with a slightly extended closing date and a two-week lease back. The buyer was happy to accommodate. They closed on the existing home, banked the money, and still had almost two and a half weeks to move remaining items out of the home because the new house was then ready to move into. They had zero homelessness because we had prepared and knew what we wanted to accomplish before we began marketing.

Russell and Melissa are a young couple with several kids. They had an older home in a wonderful part of town, but it needed quite a few repairs—everything from foundation to yard work. They just hated the idea of making repairs while living in the current home. Since they had the resources available to purchase their new home before selling their old home we identified and purchased the new home. After moving to their new home, we were able to focus on what would maximize the greatest return on the investment in the old home. Using our 7 Strategies we were able to sell their home well under the average time and for an insane amount over the average price for the area.

Step Four
Now you must prepare to buy. As Socrates has been quoted as saying, "Know Thyself." Being prepared to buy is understanding what you want. Remember Seth and Aimee. They knew their needs and were comfortable with knowing the timeline would be extended because of it.

In a seller's market you have no time to think overnight on the purchase decision. You must move quickly to get what you want and make your best offer up front. In a buyer's market the buyer usually has more time because there are more homes available, but when a house of interest comes available, I always remind my clients it is likely several other parties like it too.

When making an offer, knowing your State of Affairs is vitally important. Ask yourself if you can make a cash offer, or must it be contingent? We've all heard the old adage that "Cash is King." In a seller's market that should read "More Cash is King!"

At the time of writing, we are in the hottest seller's market in American history. It will not last forever, but it has lasted longer than anyone originally thought. The ability to make a cash offer—meaning making your offer without a mortgage—is more likely to be accepted than an offer with a mortgage contingency. You may ask "Why? My credit is good!" That may be true, but the seller wants the least number of decision-making parties involved. With a cash offer, once you and the seller agree, very few others can influence the deal negatively. With a mortgage there is an underwriter, surveyor, appraiser, and possibly many other people involved in the process who can slow or even kill the deal.

Alan and Joanna wanted to buy a property with about an acre of land, not too far out of town. They found the right place, which was still available, and they simply fell in love. While Alan and Joanna could afford to buy with cash, Alan wanted to make the offer with a mortgage, but Joanna really wanted the house. They asked me what I thought and I encouraged them to make a cash offer. Remember that currently "More Cash is King." They chose to offer $25,000 over the asking price. As it ends up, their offer was not the highest priced offer. However, their cash offer won the deal because the other higher offer involved a mortgage. During negotiations we uncovered that the seller needed an extended period to close, and it allowed Alan enough time to process the mortgage he wanted. He was prepared to bring cash if the mortgage fell through, so as not to cause a delay for closing, and it worked out great. Alan and Joanna were prepared and knew their situation well.

In any market you must have a place to live. Because of the hot seller's market in our area, Brian and Sharon decided to move into a nice apartment complex after selling their home. They hated the pressure of being in a hurry and even the slight possibility of being homeless. Even though it meant moving some things twice and placing others into storage, taking their time was a priority. The cash from the sale of their home is safely in an investment drawing interest as they decide whether to buy an existing home or to build. This worked out well for Brian and Sharon because they sat down and decided what they wanted, and what they *did not want*, and with my help we produced a game plan that satisfied their needs.

Step Five

The fifth step is understanding the mechanics of buying and selling at the same time. As we have discussed, having cash available is one of the easiest ways to make this happen smoothly. If you do not have the assets available to make a cash offer but have enough cash to make an impressive down payment, that will also strengthen your mortgaged offer greatly.

The positives of buying first is that you have a home to move into, and you only need to move once, which saves time, expense on temporary housing, and storage costs. Also, you will be under far less pressure to find a house in the brief time after your existing home goes under contract. The negatives of buying first are that you may feel rushed to sell and accept a lower offer on your existing home. If you do not have the cash or cash equivalent to buy first, you may find yourself paying two mortgages for a short while, and if you are using a contingency offer you may not find a seller willing to entertain your offers. With that said, even in a seller's market there are sellers willing to accept contingencies. Making offers is the only way to find them.

Now let's discuss the positives of selling before buying. It allows you to know exactly how much equity you will have available to pay for a new home and it is easy to roll that equity into the new purchase. Like Brian and Sharon, you may find it easier to close the chapter on the old before embarking or focusing on the next move. The negatives of selling before buying are finding a temporary home, moving some things twice, and the cost of storage which can add up fast. Knowing you can negotiate an extended closing or extended lease back and being prepared is key to maximizing any window of opportunity. Know the market, know yourself, know your options, plan, and then execute.

There is an interesting option available in some areas from companies that specialize in helping you make cash offers without selling first. There is a fee, but it may be much less than you would think. There are a couple of these companies in Texas, where I am located. When my clients have been in a situation where these companies could help, I was able to advise them and walk them through the process. Knowing your financial and overall situation and sharing it with a professional who can guide you is key.

Now, picture the final scene in a Shaggy and Scooby Doo mystery. You have moved into your new home and the villain ("The Unknown") is bound up and being taken away. You can almost hear him say, "I would have kept you out of this home if it hadn't been for that meddling John Byers and his Team!"

HOW TO WIN BIG BEFORE YOU START
GETTING FULLY PREPARED TO BUY A HOME

WITH **LEAH LITTENBERG**

After growing up in the suburbs of Los Angeles, **LEAH LITTENBERG** moved to the Dallas-Fort Worth Metroplex to attend college at Texas Christian University and never left. Her love for homes started at a young age as the daughter of a professional interior designer and her love for the home buying process started after she bought her first home in Dallas at age 23. She and husband, Alan, live in their alma mater's hometown of Fort Worth, TX, with their daughter, Janie, plus one on the way, and their three beloved dogs, Ranger, Shiner, and Hank. They are truly living out their parallel passions as Leah helps guide people through the home buying process and Alan shares his home remodel expertise through their home remodeling company, Fine Point Homes.

Leah is passionate about guiding her clients through such a personal, emotional, and stressful decision. As a natural problem-solver, she leaves no stone unturned to find her clients the right home with the best possible terms. Her diverse skill set and past experience in HR allows her to contribute to her team by bringing new ideas for how best to grow the company and care for our clients.

As TCU alumni, the Littenbergs try to attend as many TCU sporting events as they can and enjoy frequenting events that are uniquely Fort Worth.

Instagram/Facebook: @leahlittenberg
leahlittenberg@gmail.com
(817) 507-8420

HOW TO WIN BIG BEFORE YOU START
GETTING FULLY PREPARED TO BUY A HOME

Buying a home in any market can be a tough, exhausting, and stressful experience. However, if you follow this fool proof 3-step plan, it'll ensure your home buying process goes as smooth as possible.

A mutual friend introduced me to my past clients, Steve and Mary, after they had a bad experience purchasing their first home with a different realtor. They were pretty timid, frustrated, and frankly downright hesitant to purchase a new home because of what they experienced buying their first one. I was determined and knew they would have a better experience this time around because of the plan I would help put in place.

Your big why

The first thing you want to do before you even step foot into a home is to understand your core motivation. Do you have a spouse or anyone else involved in the process? You want to make sure everyone is on the same page and understands the motivation behind why you're buying this home.

So what does it actually look like to get on the same page as a spouse, or to get really clear in your own head if you're an individual buyer? There are a lot of things to think about... way beyond just about how many bedrooms and bathrooms you want.

Ask yourself: Why do I want to buy a house? Where do I want to be located? Are schools important? How far of a commute do I want to have to work?

Next you'll want to consider these questions. Do I want a home that I can renovate to completely make my own? Or do I want something that already has my dream features? And of course, what does my budget look like? What am I comfortable spending?

Believe it or not, a lot of people don't have these conversations with their spouse until they are standing in front of an agent in the middle of someone else's living room.

Do yourself a massive favor and talk through these details so you know what you're looking for ahead of time. Be aware that the specific details might change throughout your process, but it helps to at least have a good understanding of your motivation up front so you don't waste your time running around looking at houses that won't fit your needs in the long run.

Maybe you already have a really good understanding of what you're looking for. At the next level, consider things like safety and security. If one spouse travels a lot and the other will be home alone with the kids, do certain communities feel safer or more comfortable to you?

What kind of community are you deeply invested in? Are you planning on growing your family in the near future? These are the topics that buyers don't think about ahead of time, and agents who aren't world-class don't ask. Some answers actually turn out to be more important than the specific house. I always tell my clients that *where* you live dictates *how* you live, so making sure you find the neighborhood that works best for you and your family's needs is extremely important.

To get past those first couple of answers with each other, have a long discussion and dig deep on this. What did you like or not like about your past situations? Did you feel included or not included in your past neighborhood? How did you feel about the area you grew up in—what did you like and what did you not like? Would you like to live in an area that's similar or vastly different from ones you've lived in in the past?

Keep in mind that you and your partner, or whoever else is involved in this process, likely grew up in different areas and have different thoughts and opinions on what they want in this next neighborhood, so it's very important to have an open conversation about your experiences and come to a mutual understanding.

In terms of budget, remember to not let your maximum financing number determine what you can truly afford. Talk about what a comfortable monthly payment number is for you and how much cash you are willing to put toward this purchase... more on that later.

To dig even deeper, I always ask my buyers the "why." Why is it important to you to buy a home? Why is it important that you live in a certain area? Understanding your "why" ahead of time will always set you up for success. Just by asking the question, you'll realize things about yourself and what you actually want that you had never thought about before.

When Steve and Mary first sat down together with me to discuss the home buying process and what they were looking for, I asked them the hard questions. Why do you want to buy a home? They said they needed a place to live and provide for their two kids. I asked what was most important about providing for their kids, and they replied that they wanted a safe neighborhood where they would feel comfortable letting their kids play in the front yard and attend good schools. Now we're getting somewhere!

As the conversation continued, I learned that Steve didn't live in a great neighborhood growing up, so he wanted to provide something for his kids that he never had. That's a big deal! If I hadn't dug deep and asked the hard questions, we never would've known that. (And Steve likely would've never thought about the real why either!)

This information is huge when buying a home and it's immensely helpful for both you and your realtor to know these deeper motivations so that your agent can remind you, bringing you back to the bigger why when you fall in love with a "kitchen." Having this conversation immediately set Steve and Mary at ease; they were so thankful and felt instantly better about buying their second home.

Your team

The next thing you need to do is to find the best Realtor for you and your family—someone who will understand and help you find your core motivation and keep your best interest at heart throughout the entire process.

Think of it this way... if you needed brain surgery, would you consider doing the surgery yourself, or going to the neighborhood clinic? Or would you consult and interview the best surgeons in the country? Buying a home is one of, if not the biggest, financial investment you'll make in your life, so why risk making that decision all by yourself or with someone who is not an expert in the field?

So how do you even begin to find a great real estate agent? Finding the right agent to work on your behalf sets you up for success more so than any other factor in the process. You want someone who will ask you the hard questions, understand your core motivations, and keep your best interests at heart from the time you start the process until way beyond closing day.

The worst thing you can do when starting the home buying process is to find a random agent online and meet them at a home you're interested in seeing. Instead, sit down and interview agents to see who is going to be the best fit for you. Make sure they're knowledgeable about the market, are a good negotiator, and have a plan in place for you to find the right home and be competitive in your offers, without overpaying. Ask them what their processes are in certain markets, and be cautious if they don't have one.

In addition to finding a savvy and smart agent, you also want to make sure the personality fit is there. Home buying can be a long and stressful process so you want to make sure you really get along and enjoy spending time with your Realtor.

Looking at Google reviews is a great way to get honest feedback from past clients and gain insight into what it's going to be like to work with an agent. You can also ask agents to put you in touch with past clients to gain even more insight.

Don't make this decision so quickly that only one of those sources sways your decision. You can't always trust awards, trophies and rankings. And quantity doesn't necessarily mean quality. What's their track record, especially with buyers like yourself?

Another valuable thing to do is ask your Realtor friends in a different market if they know of any good Realtors in your area. Great agents have a wide network all over the country and can introduce you to an agent that they've already professionally vetted for you.

Some people think they don't need to use a realtor because they mistakenly believe that cutting out the agent might save them money, but in almost every market, that's a 100% chance of failure. It's going to cost you, even if that includes lost sleep, constant stress, fear, anxiety, and uncertainty. More than likely it will cost you money, and not just on the house, but also on future repairs you'll end up having to make because you didn't have a professional advocate on your side.

After Steve and Mary had a poor experience the first go around, they were hesitant to meet with me, and even expressed concerns to me about using an agent again. But they trusted their friend who highly recommended me and took a look at my Google reviews to get insight into who I am as a person and as a Realtor. After that first hour and a half meeting, they flat out told me how thankful they were and knew they were on the right track with me leading and guiding them through the process. They loved the game plan we set up to find homes, how to negotiate and get extra creative in order to get our offer accepted, and of course they appreciated having professional insight into the market and specific neighborhoods they were looking at. Most importantly, they felt we were a good personality fit and really appreciated that I helped them dig deeper into their motivation and knew I would help remind them of that throughout the entire process.

Your money

Last, but certainly not least, you need to figure out your financing. Are you going to be an all-cash buyer or will you finance some portion of the purchase? If financing, you will need to find a good lender who is on the same page as you. What does that look like, and what's your tolerance for budget?

It is important to make sure you're fully prepared in regard to financing your new home before you fall in love with a property that's way over your budget. This means more than just getting preapproved for a loan, or deciding you want to pay all cash. That's only a small piece of the puzzle.

To start, you need to figure out what you are comfortable spending on a monthly basis. That's the number that matters, even if a lender pre-approves you for double that. Discuss your monthly household budget and ensure you have a number that will not stretch you thin, making you "house poor." You also want to discuss how much cash to close you are comfortable putting down. A lot of people only think about the down payment on the home, but you also need to include the price of closing costs which are typically 3-4% of the purchase price.

Agents often have a preferred lender they can refer you to, those they have worked with time and time again and have a great track record. What makes a great lender goes beyond just getting the best interest rate. You always want to work with a local lender, not an online or national bank. This will go a long way when getting your offer accepted, especially in a multiple-offer situation.

There are a number of questions you can ask to help you decide between lenders. How quickly can they close? How accessible are they? Can you reach out to them on a Saturday morning when you find the house you want to put in an offer? Are they going to be able to call the listing agent on your behalf to help elevate your offer?

If instead you're looking at an all-cash buy, make sure to set your boundaries and understand your tolerance for budget. How much are you willing to spend? You still have to pay property taxes and homeowners insurance each year, which will be directly correlated with purchase price, size, and age of home. You also want to consider the age of the roof, HVAC, hot water heater and other items that might need to be replaced over time.

Whatever you decide, you will need to have full preapproval if you're financing or have a proof of funds statement from your bank or a letter from your lawyer if you're planning on doing all cash, before you start your search. If you wait to get this until after you've fallen in love with your dream home, that home will likely already be gone by the time you're able to collect a preapproval or proof of funds letter.

If you have the ability to purchase with cash, you may want to consider financing depending on interest rates, the current market, and your overall wealth building strategy. In some markets, you might want to put all of your cash into the home purchase because your cash may be losing value elsewhere. Or you might choose to put a slightly lower down payment on a home because you're going to use the additional cash for repairs and build equity faster that way.

Thinking through your strategy upfront is powerful. Often it sounds like cash is always better, but for some long-term wealth building strategies, it's not. The lowest interest rate may seem like it is always best, but for some timetables, it's not. Make sure you're discussing your timetable and long-term goals with your lender so they can help guide you to making the best decision for your overall financial goals. Most people don't think beyond interest rate and wind up missing out on greater wealth in the long run.

When paying cash, another item to consider is the appraisal. You will not be required to purchase an appraisal as a cash buyer, however, you may still want to get the property appraised because that provides an authoritative third-party challenge to a purchase price. It can alert you when you may be overpaying, or cheer you on to know you're getting a great deal. It's also a terrific negotiation tool. If you get a low appraisal, you can come back to negotiate the price with the seller.

Again, there is lots to unpack with financing, but having these conversations internally, with your lender or trusted financial advisors is all very important, and most importantly done ahead of falling in love with a home so that you don't make a rushed decision that you regret down the line. According to a Business Insider survey published in February 2022, 64% of home buyers regretted buying their home, mostly due to the fact that they felt rushed into making a decision. That buyer remorse could have been alleviated if they had better prepared and done the hard work ahead of time.

Steve and Mary went with my trusted lender recommendation, Patrick, and were beyond thrilled with the results. He walked them through all of their options, and suggested a few things they had never even thought of, which they highly appreciated. When we found "the one" they were fully prepared with their preapproval letter,

Patrick called the listing agent on their behalf and we won even in a multiple-offer situation. They were absolutely over the moon! Steve and Mary now introduce me to as many people as they can because of the great experience they had purchasing a home with me, and we've become close friends in the process. This example is one of many reasons behind why I got into real estate and why I love what I do day in and day out.

Home buying can be a rollercoaster of a process if you're not prepared, however, if you have these deep, hard conversations up front, understand your core motivation, find the best realtor for your needs, and figure out your financing well in advance, you will set yourself up to win big and have a successful and smooth home buying experience.

BUYING A SECOND HOME IN A LIFESTYLE OR DESTINATION MARKET

WITH GARRETT & DONNA SANDELL

GARRETT and **DONNA SANDELL** are from a small town in South Central Kansas at the edge of Flint Hills, Winfield, Kansas. They grew up in the surrounding area and raised their families there. Donna has sold real estate since 1993 and Garrett worked in the automotive industry. They love the sunshine and "Salt Life" lifestyle and were frequently drawn to Florida.

Garrett and Donna joined Keller Williams in 2013 and service the Marco Island/Naples areas. They enjoy meeting new people from all over the world and helping them discover everything that Southwest Florida has to offer.

They work together to prepare and guide you through the buying and selling process, as well as help you navigate and disseminate the overwhelming amount of information. They strive to be the pinnacle of a great customer experience.

Their mission is to educate, inform and serve.
—"Livin' the Dream Team"

www.teamsandellswfl.com
teamsandellswfl@gmail.com
(239) 682-7600

BUYING A SECOND HOME IN A LIFESTYLE OR DESTINATION MARKET

Buying real estate for our daily lives is something most people have done, but when you think more aspirationally about retirement or a second home in a vacation destination, you get the privilege and opportunity to start dreaming more about your ideal lifestyle... without the burdens and daily obligations of your usual grind.

With that joy comes a very different approach to home buying. How do you want to spend your days after your new purchase? Strolling the beach for seashells after your morning coffee? Golfing 18 holes with new friends? Fishing the Gulf of Mexico or the backwaters in the Everglades? Maybe painting at the art center or exploring nearby art galleries. How about volunteering at a nature center or teaching children about wildlife and how we humans affect the environment.

Getting clear on your dreams

What have you been dreaming about for the last 20 years? We all dream about what life might be like after retirement, but do we really dig into what that will mean on a day-to-day basis?

As Americans, we've been spoiled by having lots of options, so it's hard to make just one choice. We tend to gravitate toward a little bit of this and a little bit of that, without ever creating a really clear vision.

For many people who want a second home or vacation home or retirement home, they still haven't fully developed an understanding of the lifestyle they want to create.

In our Southwest Florida market, we see not only snowbirds looking for a second home, but also those searching for a home in advance of life-changing events. For some that means kids graduating from college, and for others it's someone who is about to sell the family business. It takes that life-changing event before they begin to think seriously about making a change.

It takes time to wrap your head around making such a next step. This is frequently the moment when we get the opportunity to meet with the person or couple. One of our specialties is helping you develop an idea of what you would like the next phase of your life to be like. That's where we come in to help guide you to that dream.

A little advice from someone who's been there

Most people spend years building wealth while dreaming about a vacation home. But they actually never get clarity on what they want that home to do for them. Is it purely financial? Is it a lifestyle? What do you want this house to do for you? Think about it... and ask yourself some questions. At the end of the day what do you really want?

Helping you through the transition

Here on Marco Island and the Naples, Florida area, when we meet clients and go explore the possibilities, it's usually amazing that after they purchase, they can pull their car into the driveway, walk through their new home, then hop on a boat and be in the Gulf inside of five minutes. Sometimes it takes a while for them to wrap their head around all that. It's pretty amazing to watch them start to smile. We get to help families achieve something they didn't even realize was possible.

The home you've been dreaming of in your mind hasn't necessarily connected all the dots yet. Maybe you've fantasized about having a nice water view from your new Florida condo, but you've likely never thought about whether you want to be able to walk straight out the door onto the beach or climb into your boat on the canal where you can cruise out to one of the area's 10,000 islands for a quite remote afternoon.

Once you begin to envision the lifestyle you want, it becomes easier to go out and find a home that will fulfill your true dreams.

Older buyers may be interested in proximity to hospitals or our award-winning resort style senior living communities. Snowbirds often want to know about nearby airports. For those who have families up north, you will want to know how quickly you can get a car service or get back home for a family holiday. Here in Southwest Florida we have four airports within two hours driving distance and two executive airports for private jets, so that offers a wide variety of options.

We also get a lot of questions regarding property care when the owner can't be present. Many are surprised to learn that in our area, there's a "car condo" where you can store your dream car in air-conditioned, climate-controlled luxury. (More about that later.)

After you get really clear on your vision of what you want your life to look like, next ask yourself what you want to do recreationally. Do you want to golf? Become a foodie? Work on getting more fit or healthy? Relax and read a really good book poolside? Listen to live music under the Tiki Bar at happy hour? Travel extensively?

Another consideration is how you want to use the home. Will you be retiring immediately, or not for five years? Are you purchasing as an investment? Will you be living in the property fulltime or for a partial year? The answers to these questions make a big difference.

Some buyers purchase a property initially to get into the area, then once they actually move in and settle into life, they refine where they want to be. But they've hedged their money because they're already in this market. Many times we've helped people buy, then sell, then buy again, getting to that perfect spot for their new lives... and often it is quite different than what they originally envisioned.

Getting clear on what supports your dream

This second part of achieving the dream may not be as fun as fantasizing about playing 36 holes of golf on a weekday, but it's a step that will make all the difference in your success and happiness of your home purchase. Most people fail to think about how to make sure the dream really happens.

Think about the needs-based activities that will be real in your life. How do you play 36 holes a day? Well, you need to store your clubs. Do you want a golf cart? What do you do about off-season vehicle storage, tools, equipment, or property management? If you're going to lease your home, do you hire a cleaning service?

You can have a driver pick you up at the airport, then drop you right at your home. But what about groceries and supplies? Actually, there is a service for that, too. The fridge and pantry can be all stocked up, and your mini fridge can be filled with your favorite adult beverages. The lights will be on and the house clean and tidy. Your pool will be sparkling and ready to jump into. Best of all, the boat can be on the dock, gassed up and ready for adventure.

There are home-watch and cleaning services as well as those who do grocery shopping for you. Other options include folks who check your home when needed to make sure the A/C is running properly and everything is just like you left it. There are marinas to store your boat, car condos to keep your car in air-controlled storage, and of course with technology, you can also set up a "smart" home and monitor your house from your phone, wherever you are in the world. Peace of mind when you're not using this property comes from having all the services provided that you need.

Two approaches to achieving your dream second home

Once you've gotten clear on what you want and how you want to live—and the services needed to support that lifestyle—now it's time to talk about the funds and your timing to identify what's available on the existing market, or where you can build new construction.

There's also a methodical approach we help people take that allows them to move here full-time, then pick a specific area or neighborhood later. Many people's lifestyle changes dramatically once they relocate. You might realize you really enjoy boating more than golfing or fishing. This could lead you to decide you want a home on the canal so you can own your own boat.

Maybe you buy a starter property, then sell it and upgrade to another. While you're doing that, you get a real feel for the area and the kind of life you want to live there, whether it's in retirement or vacation or just a second home.

Once you've gotten to know the area more intimately, and maybe made money on a couple of buy/sells, then you can put all that learning and resources into one final purchase of a dream home with all the fun, sexy, exciting stuff, knowing you have a firm grip on all the necessary support material and the financial resources to enjoy it.

Most communities in Naples have a more affordable, but totally approachable entry point. People will buy there and might sell later to upgrade, or they might keep this home forever because it's always desirable. There are beautiful, gated communities that match any lifestyle.

The possibilities are endless—from having your private driver pick you up after landing on your private jet, taking you to your home on the Gulf of Mexico, or having an amazing investment property that produces six figures a year on the oceanfront.

The bottom line

It's your dream; dare to imagine it. You are the one who decides what that is going to be. Finding the right professional to get there is important, as it is a lifetime investment you are making. There are lots of real estate agents but very few Realtors with the knowledge and experience you can trust to make it happen.

SECRET AND SUCCESSFUL NEGOTIATING STRATEGIES

WITH LESLIE STEWART

LESLIE STEWART was born and raised in Las Vegas, and has witnessed the extreme changes in the real estate market over the years. A product of the Clark County School District, she is a graduate of the original Las Vegas High School downtown campus and earned her degree from the University of Nevada, Las Vegas, in real estate. This city is Leslie's home, and she has worked to help others find their homes for over a decade. In fact, she is among the top 5% of real estate agents in the valley.

When buying a home, she zones in on the details of her client's needs, stays in constant communication, and leverages her vast network to find the perfect home. Her negotiating skill when submitting offers has a winning track record when there are multiple offers. Sellers know her experience will help them sell their home quickly and hassle-free. The Stewart Team has a process to help sellers prepare their homes for sale, resulting in offers above the average price and in less time than the industry standard. More than a job, real estate is her passion.

Leslie and her husband of 25 years are both natives of Las Vegas and have four children and two mini Dachshunds. She is an active member of her church and the Scottish Celtic community. She currently serves on the board for the Las Vegas Highland Dance Association and the Las Vegas Pipe Band.

www.stewartlvrealestate.com
leslie@stewartlvrealestate.com
(702) 526-3404

SECRET AND SUCCESSFUL NEGOTIATING STRATEGIES

Most people have a movie scene in mind when they think of the word "negotiation." They picture a life-or-death hostage negotiation, tactics implemented to avoid a world war, or an intense boardroom scene in a New York high-rise. This is what most people think negotiation is, but this is how I define it: anything which affects your time, money or stress level.

When purchasing a home, fortunately, negotiation doesn't have to have such a cinematic element of conflict, but we can apply a few lessons to our situation. One of the keys to negotiation is to recognize that each party will have their own perception coming into the transaction and recognize that reality is now our joint circumstance. Unless a buyer has an agent with expertise, it can be challenging to navigate these circumstances and you could miss out on key leverage points which would have created advantages and an overall better buying experience.

Over the years, I've enjoyed helping home buyers to skillfully and respectfully navigate the purchase process using these powerful but not necessarily difficult strategies to get a great deal on their home.

5 Strategies for Success

Negotiations are not always about the price. There are other terms and conditions that can be negotiated to get the best outcome. I'm going to share my five secret and successful strategies with you. You'll find none of them are complex, but you will be surprised how underutilized they are. People generally view negotiation as black and white... and hard. In a home-buying scenario, this isn't how it has to be and knowing how to be creative is essential to good negotiation.

Strategy #1: What is the seller's situation?

Let's recognize that this first strategy occurs in any market condition, as the engagement with the seller side begins. You will want to find out what the seller's pain points are and how to tactically alleviate them. Finding the cure will put you in an advantageous position and essentially this allows you to look like the superstar, saving them from the misery of selling their house.

For example, some sellers, may want their money fast, but with the option to move out slow. Perhaps they are relocating and need to sell in order to purchase their next home and a presenting a leaseback provides that flexibility, This could put your offer in a highly favorable position. For other sellers, their ideal buyer will appreciate all the home and community has afforded them over the years. In some cases, this aspect is more important to them than the money or the speed. If you are aware of these deeper considerations, it will help you craft exactly the right offer to win their hearts... and ultimately the home of your dreams.

Being able to discover and identify the seller's concerns gives the buyer an opportunity to provide value outside of the purchase price, such as an extended close of escrow or mitigating repair request fears.

Not reaching out to the seller's side in an attempt to gather information on their circumstances prior to writing your offer could be the sole reason you don't even get the opportunity to purchase the property. Let this serve as a cautionary tale, for buyers, if you or your agent dismiss this strategy.

Strategy #2 How long has the property been on the market?

In any given market, there's going to be an average number of days for how long a house remains on the market. It could be a lot, or it could be a little. Allow this to determine your amount of available leverage.

If the home has been listed for longer than the market average, you can use this knowledge to leverage your offer to encourage the win for the seller while saving you some money.

If instead, the home has been on the market for a below-average number of days, acknowledge that the seller has more leverage. As a buyer, you need to know how work around that.

Essentially, this strategy allows you to know when to loosen the reins and when to tighten them.

The typical individual who's buying or selling a home has, at best, a ballpark idea of the length of time to expect a home to stay on the market. But bear in mind this might be totally irrelevant when considering a specific property type or neighborhood or block. An algorithm can't calculate the perceived value difference between neighborhoods zoned in a certain school district or located next to a freeway.

These considerations play a huge role in how competitive this particular property will be.

If the average days on market in an area is 48, and you're seeing the property on Day 2, you need to recognize that you really don't have a ton of leverage. However, if you're touring the home on Day 148, you can shoot for the stars.

Strategy #3: Timing

A lot of attention is given to money when buying a home, where nowhere near enough attention is paid to the value of your time. As you approach negotiating your next home purchase, consider that time is often a more limited resource than money for many sellers.

Some sellers will be enticed by a shorter inspection period or prefer tight appraisal or financial conditions. Sometimes responding quickly gives you more leverage, while other times being slower and more methodical is an advantage. Perhaps, using your fully allotted timeframe on in the due diligence or option period creates a better path.

The element of timing can be used a lot of different ways in different situations. It may seem that sellers have the control when it comes to timeframes and deadlines, but buyers can use them to their advantage as well.

For example, when you make an offer or counteroffer, giving the seller a deadline to reply can help get a quick response and decisions can be made. This will also let the seller know you are ready to move forward and are serious.

Some sellers need to sell yesterday. Whether they're in financial trouble, going through a bankruptcy, dealing with a divorce, or moving out of state, many sellers want shortened time frames and a quick close.

For other sellers, they may place importance on financial security. Having earnest money sent to title quickly or appraisal or loan contingencies removed in a timely manner will help move your purchase along in the best way possible.

Time is of the essence and using it to leverage your position with sellers can give you the upper hand.

Strategy #4: Equity opportunities

A highly powerful way to deepen the above strategy is to go eyes wide open and identify those properties that will allow you to create your own equity because they have been less competitive on the market. Intentionally seek out properties that may have been on the market a little longer. Perhaps they have outdated finishes, but the integrity of your prime location and floor plan are intact. This allows you to look at homes that may appear, on the surface, to be beyond your price point, but after negotiations will fall right in your budget since the seller is likely more inclined to drop price after a frustrating length of time on the market.

This equity opportunity gives you a chance to negotiate in the cost of what it will take to have the property renovated to suit you. You'll get be able to install updated finishes of your choice and thereby increase the value of the property when you decide to sell later.

It also may allow greater financing opportunities. If ever you want to refinance to lower your debt to loan value, you can leverage PMI savings or home equity credit opportunities when buying a home this way.

The negotiation strategy of identifying a home like this is that you can be more aggressive with price terms and seller concessions. It is an acquired skill to clearly communicate to the seller that the home is not at top value or maximum equity in its current, as-is state. With eloquence and tact being able to address the current condition of the home and the areas which need of attention can help sellers recognize their reality and provide the equity opportunity for you.

For example, maybe you're viewing a home that's currently a "7" out of 10, but it has obvious potential to become a full "10." As you make the initial inquiry and give feedback, identify, acknowledge, and communicate the gap to the seller or their agent as the starting point for future negotiations.

Potentially quantify the value cost between those two points.

Strategy #5: Don't let ego or emotion get in the way of your dream home

When purchasing a home, especially your primary residence, recognize it's different than entering a business transaction. Your home will represent security and safety. It's where your family is going to reside, spend time together, and make memories.

But at the same time, keep your objective top of mind. Why are you looking for a home in the first place? You began the journey with a clear purpose and vision, not to emerge victorious over a seller. This process is not about the perception of the buyer or seller winning or losing. It's about moving your life forward to the chapter where you own and live in the home of your dreams.

Very few aspects of this negotiation will last long-term. What you're going to take with you in the future has nothing to do with the particular individual who owned the home before you got there. Keep the focus instead on how to get the deal done so you can move on and create the amazing life you have envisioned your new home.

Rather than trying to put down the lender, the appraiser, the surveyor, or the terrible way an inspection was communicated—which in the short-term creates significant emotions and drama that won't last—stay focused on what does last. Focus on your core principles and values, and the benefits of owning the home and growing your life forward.

I'm sure you've heard horror stories where a homeowner rants that because they had to pay their buyer's closing costs, that's how it has to operate on their next purchase, so the seller of the home they want needs to pay their closing costs. In truth, the two situations are totally unrelated.

Look at what lasts. What house do you get? If this home will be your primary residence, allow for a bit more personal emotion and dreaming, but still acknowledge that this is a significant financial investment. The timing and pricing will definitely impact your decision.

This is one of the many places where having a world-class realtor on your team will help protect you. They're not going to jump in the family swimming pool with you, but they can advise and give you objectivity on specific situations they've negotiated a hundred times before.

As a real estate agent, I understand this element, but when my husband and I recently purchased our home, we had to apply this strategy. My spouse who works in an entirely different industry, was concerned about different details. We had to regroup our focus on the big picture and recognize that increasing our offer gave us additional leverage with the seller and allowed us to buy in an area we desired with a park right behind our house. It was everything we wanted, and when spread out over a 30-year mortgage at a great interest rate, the overall difference in our monthly expense was negligible.

Maintaining objectivity during the home-buying process is very difficult to do if you're the only decision maker and information gatherer. This is another great reason so many people rely on a real estate professional. It allows you to garner insight from a neutral third party who can be your unbiased advocate.

In summary, these 5 secret and successful negotiating strategies are tactics most buyers don't even think about and are certainly underutilized. When employed together, these methods can create advantages you didn't realize were even options in your home buying process. You will also be able to increase your leverage and improve the terms of the contract in any market condition so you can enjoy the process of buying a home significantly more.

Bonus

For my list of 17 other items besides price to negotiate in your next home purchase, visit URL

WHAT YOU NEED TO KNOW WHEN IT COMES TO BUYING NEW CONSTRUCTION

WITH MARI ARSTEIN

MARI ARSTEIN initially started her career in real estate in San Antonio before moving to Fort Worth to join the Todd Tramonte Home Selling Team as a buyer's specialist. Thanks to her skill set and background in retail sales, management and human resources, she consistently delivers professional and quality service while educating, guiding, and serving her clients through the home buying process.

Mari sets a high standard for herself and is constantly seeking to grow and refine her craft as an expert in the industry. Her passion for helping people take advantage of the incredible opportunities finding a new home provides drives her to meet the needs of her clients. Whether it's her clients, fellow team members, friends or family, Mari genuinely cares for people and seeks to help and add value any way that she can. She is the quintessential team player. She loves the friendly people, culture, and small town charm that Fort Worth offers without sacrificing the amenities of the big city.

www.myfortworthmls.com
mari@toddtramonte.com
(253) 330-3764

WHAT YOU NEED TO KNOW WHEN IT COMES TO BUYING NEW CONSTRUCTION

Many people don't realize that there are a lot of differences between purchasing new construction versus a pre-owned home—everything from how to go about searching for a home to the technical and logistical aspects of the transaction process.

For instance, when searching for a home, people often like to browse on Zillow or Realtor.com, or they may have their agent give them access to the local MLS. This works if you are searching for a pre-owned home, but won't give you many results if you are going the new-build route.

The technical and logistical differences between a pre-owned process and a new construction process are also important to be aware of before starting your house hunt. Many people think, "Okay, let's go buy a new house today!" Then they go straight to a builder, sign on the dotted line, and then find out what's really involved only later. Whether you use an agent or go it alone, having this approach without being fully prepared will not set you up for success.

One simple example of a logistical difference between pre-owned and new construction that you need to think about is timeline. You can buy a resale home within 30-40 days, but new construction usually takes 6-18 months, depending on market conditions. Rarely is there one just sitting waiting. So, before diving in, know your own timeline demands so that you can make decisions best for you, your family, and your finances. This chapter will give you an overview of all the things to consider when you and your family are interested in purchasing new construction.

Locating new construction homes

Next, how do you find new-build homes that are for sale?

Your main options are the MLS, resource websites, and builder-specific websites. If you're working with an agent, they can give you access to the MLS database which sometimes will have new-builds listed from various builders. Keep in mind that these listings are sometimes just a placeholder for what might be available in the future. The real house might not even be built yet. Their list prices are also just an estimate and not always accurate to the actual property it represents, or the amenities your newly constructed might include.

Working with a real estate agent who specializes in new construction will typically be your most accurate source of information, because they have regular conversations with builder representatives and will be able to do the heavy-lifting of checking listings for accuracy. If your agent sends you an MLS listing for a new build, it is good to indicate whether or not you are interested so that your agent can contact the builder directly to get specifics and accurate information, or fine-tune their searches for you in the future.

In some areas, there are resource websites like BuilderGuides.com or New Home Source. Websites like these are typically available for specific markets so you will want to research what website would be a tool for your area. This will give you an overview of what communities are being built with what builder. It's not all encompassing, and it's not always up to date though. Sometimes they'll list communities that have already been closed out, or ones that are coming in the future, but it is a valuable tool you can use to get started. Then, verify the information you've found with the builder directly. Again, if you are working with an agent, they can take on the heavy-lifting of contacting each builder to get details on availability, timing, and price.

Each builder will likely also have a website. While you probably have heard of the big building companies, your agent may also know of some smaller, less well-known builders in your specific market. Definitely ask your agent about all the other builders out there, and then visit their websites to see their inventory level. Again, you or your agent can call on your behalf and verify information found on the website, because these are not always kept up to date. Depending on market conditions, availability, pricing, estimated completion dates can change rapidly. My recommendation would be that while you or your agent are on the phone with the builder, schedule a meeting with the builder representative, where you can ask questions, see the model homes, and get a feel for the specific builder's style.

There was a client of mine who really wanted a new construction home. We had visited with multiple builders and eventually met with one that had a floorplan coming in the near future that checked all the boxes. According to their website, the product was available now, but when I spoke with the builder representative, we were informed that a purchase agreement could not be signed until the floorplan had been released by corporate. At the time, we were in an extreme seller's market where many builders had waitlists and weren't allowing purchase agreements to be signed until the home had reached a certain level of completion. So my client and I decided we would call the builder every day to see if the home had been released to get under contract. My client ended up getting under contract on the property and was thrilled! As he was signing the purchase agreement, the builder representative commented multiple times on how the second the property was released she knew to contact us first since we had been the squeaky wheel. All that is to say that websites are not always able to give the full story on what is required to get that home, and if using a real estate agent, they are there to help you and go to bat for you.

How the buying process differs

Now let's dig into the differences in the process of buying a new build versus a pre-owned home. The first one is inventory. With a pre-owned home, you have a lot of variety like the age of the house, the neighborhoods and locations, and the materials used. If you're looking at new construction, however, not only will the choice of neighborhood and location be limited to where they are building the new communities, but the floorplans will be more rigid as well, unless you do a build-on-your-lot customized home. Builders, typically have a handful of floorplans that you can choose from. They may offer some structural customization options like ceiling height or adding an extra bedroom in lieu of the study, but overall they are fairly templated. You will need to determine if the available floorplans are what you are looking for and work for your lifestyle.

When it comes to the age of new builds, obviously new homes will have been built within a year or two of when you sign the purchase agreement, and pre-owned homes will vary in age. That's pretty straightforward. But the timeline of when you can move into your home is quite a bit different. A pre-owned home typically closes in 30-45 days once a contract is executed, while new builds take 6-18 months on average, depending on if you are purchasing an inventory home or if it is being built from the ground up. Take into consideration how this timing will fit into your timeframe.

I had some clients who had been looking during a market phase where new builds had waitlists. Both inventory and timing were big obstacles. As their agent, I constantly performed searches on their behalf and contacted different builders to find options. There was a builder I had worked with earlier in the year who had a property already under construction. This home would be finished within the buyer's timeframe, and it even had all the features they were looking for. My client, the builder, and I stayed in contact throughout the process and they were even able to close a month early. If you'd like to experience the joys of new home ownership, it's not only possible, but it's worth it if you or your agent can have the diligence of finding the right fit.

In terms of inventory availability, obviously there are more existing homes. That's one of the big reasons why more people buy pre-owned. Another is that most people aren't interested in waiting a year or more. And of course they don't want to have to deal with all those overwhelming decisions. They consider it far easier to buy what's already available. But don't let the smaller inventory scare you off. If the timing works well, and you are excited to make your vision a reality, a new build home can be an incredible experience.

As you may already know, when purchasing a pre-owned home, you have a buyer, a buyer's agent, a seller, and a listing agent. The listing agent's loyalty is to the seller. The offer gets coordinated with the seller through that listing agent, just like the buyer's agent represents the buyer and works with the buyer's best interests in mind. Similarly, a purchase agreement for a new-build home is coordinated through a builder representative. Whether you do the process on your own or with a buyer's agent, it is important to be aware that the builder representative's loyalty is to the builder. On top of that, a listing agent for a pre-owned home still has some ethical obligations to treat you with honesty and clarity and decency... but the builder rep does not. They're rarely a licensed agent and almost never a member of an association with ethical requirements, therefore they don't have the same licensing standards holding them accountable.

This isn't to say that all builder representatives are sketchy or out to con you. In fact, I have worked with many polite, friendly, helpful ones. However, their job is to look out for the builder's best interests, not yours. In fact, just the other day, my client called me and told me that he was upset because the countertops that had been installed were not the same as what he was told when he signed the purchase agreement. The builder representative had accidentally miscommunicated what was being put into the house. The builder rep told my client that, because of the market, they weren't going to do anything about it even though it was their mistake. If my client backed out, they could easily get a new buyer and he would have to pay more for the same house because of the increase in market value. Part of my job is to go to bat for my client, so I called and convinced them to take the matter to people higher up the ladder to find a solution. Make sure that you have an authoritative expert in your corner, whether that be yourself or your agent.

Contract differences

Another logistical difference between a pre-owned and new construction home is in the contract itself. In pre-owned, there is a standardized contract that all real estate agents use. With a builder however, their team of attorneys creates the document. So each builder's purchase agreement is going to be slightly different. You need to know what to look out for. For example, in an extreme seller's market, there are sometimes clauses in new-construction contracts where the builder can raise prices due to a rising cost of materials. If you, as a buyer, have not read through that in detail, your purchase price may raise significantly during the build time. In the past, the purchase price has risen so dramatically that buyers could no longer afford the house they were under contract for. They had to back out of the deal and start from square one in an ever-changing market. As you can imagine, this created hardship for the buyer both financially and emotionally.

Reading the builder's contract thoroughly is extremely important. Sometimes, even if you did read it but aren't familiar with how builders interpret certain line items, you could still get yourself in trouble. It isn't always as clear and obvious as you might think. A wise option is to have someone, like an agent who specializes in new construction, to read through this with you. Builders are not necessarily trying to take advantage of you, but again, they are there to protect their interests and maintain a decent profit, so you really will benefit from having a representative who will make sure that you are entering into the transaction fully knowledgeable.

Go direct?

You may be wondering if it's possible or wise to go direct to the builder and manage the whole process by yourself. You certainly can, but it's rarely recommended. As we have already discussed, it's important to have an agent who will have your back and make sure you are equipped with all the information you need in each step.

Another thing that people don't always think about is the need for transparent communication. I had a friend who went out browsing new-build homes and decided to sign a purchase agreement that same day. They didn't realize that once they signed without informing the builder that they were using a real estate agent, they were not allowed to have an agent represent them in the process moving forward. The transaction ended up being a very stressful experience for them because they didn't know who to call with their questions, or even what questions to ask, and they were not getting updates like the builder had promised.

Know that if you plan to have an agent, be sure to inform the builder before signing a purchase agreement. This way your agent will be able to represent you throughout the process and be your guide and advocate. They can communicate questions and issues to the various contacts associated with building your property, including everyone from the project manager to the builder rep, the lender and the title company.

What to ask

With new construction, "finding a deal" revolves around really knowing what questions to ask. Questions like…

- Are there incentives for taking action on certain timelines or by using the builder's preferred lender?
- What kind of deposits are necessary, and when are those deposits due?
- What are the deadlines for making structural and design changes?
- What features come standard and what are upgraded?
- How many of the available lots have lot premiums and why?

Once you have answers to these and other questions, you can begin to form more realistic ideas about the builder and make decisions about what will best suit your future.

The unexpected

One unexpected cost area of new construction involves something called the design center. If you are having a home built from the ground up, you will have an appointment at the design center where you will be able to pick your cabinets, flooring, countertops, front door, and more. One mistake people make in this step is assuming that what they saw in the model home is already factored into the initial purchase price. In reality, there are several different levels of countertops, cabinets, etc. The ones in the model homes (or what you have pictured in your mind) are often a higher level and come with an upcharge.

When meeting with the builder, have them give you as much information as possible about what comes "standard" with the home. Are blinds included? Does the home automatically have gutters installed? What are the standard ceiling heights? Another question to ask is, "How much does the average person spend at the design center?" This will help with knowing what your overall purchase price will be when all is said and done.

Having an agent on your team can be useful at this stage as well, because as you determine what things to add on or upgrade, they can give you insight into whether it will be more cost-effective to have the builder install the item or contract it to a third-party crew after closing. Real Estate agents often have contacts for various vendors that they can pass along to you, or even reach out to get quotes on your behalf.

For example, the builder may not automatically install blinds throughout your house, but this can be added for $X amount. Your agent may know Joe of Joe Blinds who can install them for $Y amount after the house has been closed on. Sometimes builders charge far and above market price for "upgrades." They are, after all, in business to make a profit. But you can think outside the box as far as your options to achieve the same end result. By comparing and contrasting extra expenses that appear later in the process, it can often save you a great deal of money.

Choosing a lender

The same idea goes for picking a lender. Oftentimes, the builder will offer an incentive to use their preferred lender and/or title company. It may cover an allowance at the design center, or a portion of closing costs, or paying for the title policy. There are times when taking advantage of this is worthwhile, but there are times when it is not. It is important to compare and contrast various lenders to see what their rates are, their fees, timeline, and so on. While the incentives for using the builder's preferred lender and title company can be enticing, you may end up sacrificing time or energy down the road.

I had a client who decided to use the builder's title company. When it came time to close, the title company kept changing the closing time and location to adjust to whatever was most convenient for them. My client and I ended up having to drive to a location an hour away and she had to take additional time off work to accommodate the changing closing time. It was clear the title company had no loyalty to my client. For some, the inconvenience is worth the incentive, but for others it is not. This is a question to ask yourself and think through what you prefer in advance.

Getting the best price

Now that you know all this, what good does it do you? New construction can be a great option for your next home as long as you stay focused and diligent when working with builders.

There is a myth out there that if you work without a real estate agent, you can get a better sales price. The reasoning behind it is that the builder would not need to pay out commission to an agent, so they should be willing to give you a better deal. In reality, the builder has already worked in the cost of an agent's compensation into their price... and that price doesn't change. So if you go in without an agent, it simply means the builder will get to keep more profit. Remember this detail and don't let that be a factor when deciding if you are going to have an agent represent you in the new-construction process.

Many people don't buy new construction. They find it easier, simpler, and just honestly more familiar to buy an existing home. But don't let the potential complexity and differences keep you from having the joy of owning a brand new home that has only ever belonged to you. It can be a really, really wonderful thing. It is totally doable if you follow these steps and have a strategic plan in place, especially if you leverage the power of a professional real estate agent to help you negotiate all the detailed aspects of the process.

INSTITUTIONAL INVESTING
5 WAYS TO REDUCE RISK & MAXIMIZE PROFITS IN TODAY'S MARKET

WITH MICHAEL ODEN

MICHAEL ODEN, affectionately known as M.O., is the founder and managing broker at Dream Home Today. His mission is to educate, equip, and empower the real estate dreams of others. Since 2002, Michael and his "dream team" have successfully guided private individuals, private equity groups, for-profit and non-profit developers through the complexities of over 400 real estate transactions. Most notable is Michael's ability to build mutually beneficial relationships and execute win-win negotiations. Michael's passion "MHAA" — Making Housing Affordable Again — has his team focused on helping developers in the Southeast U.S. address the shortage of affordable housing for low-to-moderate income citizens.

Michael's previous entrepreneurial experiences include founding Eminent Properties, LLC, an investment firm specializing in residential and commercial real estate in Cobb County, GA, owning and operating five ATC Income Tax locations serving the tax needs of over 1,100 Metro Atlanta residents, and operating a CleanNet USA franchise, one of the nation's largest commercial cleaning companies. Also, Michael has worked for several Fortune 500 Companies including Kimberly Clark, Ford Motor, John Deere, Intel, and Kraft Foods.

Besides his professional endeavors, Michael has a heart for service. As a dedicated member of the Atlanta Urban League Young Professionals, Michael was selected 2008 Southern Region member of the year for his community service efforts. Also, Michael is an alumni of LEAD Atlanta, which is an eight-month leadership training program conducted by Leadership Atlanta.

Michael is a native of Detroit, MI, and a proud Alumni of Michigan State University. He currently resides in Marietta, GA, with his wife Dr. Ayana Oden, his daughters Gabrielle and Mackenzie, and their loving yorkies, Napoleon and Zeus.

www.dreamhometoday.net
mo@dreamhometoday.net
(678) 551-6608

INSTITUTIONAL INVESTING
5 WAYS TO REDUCE RISK & MAXIMIZE PROFITS IN TODAY'S MARKET

The world of real estate has embarked upon a new day. Long gone are the days of only the "Rich and Famous" or "Old Money" making wildly profitable real estate investments. Today's world is packed full of *fintech* (financial technology) and *proptech* (property technology) solutions that enable for-profit and non-profit organizations to syndicate market expertise, financial resources and operational expertise to acquire, develop and deploy real estate assets.

Within just a few short years we've witnessed small technology organizations turn into real estate giants... Zillow, Opendoor, and Offerpad to name just a few. Billion-dollar private equity groups like Blackstone, who once deemed investing in single-family housing a game reserved for the "Mom and Pop" investors, now buy single-family homes by the thousands... hundreds of thousands to be exact... with no plans to stop in sight.

The world of real estate investing has changed. It's transitioned into a world full of Institutional Investors who are focused on meeting the demand for affordable housing in the U.S., while minimizing risk and maximizing profits for shareholders. But the question remains... how do Institutional Investors minimize risk and maximize profits in today's hyper-competitive market?

As a real estate investor, developer, and broker for 20 years I've seen individuals and institutional investors alike make similar mis-steps when it comes to real estate investing. In most instances, these mistakes are easily preventable. Based on research and real world experience, my team and I have identified five ways your organization can reduce risk and maximize profits in today's real estate market.

What's your buy box?

In real estate you make your profit when you buy, not when you sell. Institutional investors need to be very strategic about what they're trying to accomplish and how they go about accomplishing their goals. It's imperative to establish a "Buy Box" to steer your firm's decision-making when it comes to investment opportunities. Without one, you're putting your resources at risk. And most importantly, you're putting your profitability and your shareholder's return at risk, too.

Your firm's Buy Box provides the management team with several critical parameters to use when making investment decisions. It answers questions like: "Will your firm buy existing developed stock or raw land for development?" It determines which financing resources will be used to acquire investments. It lays out your disposition strategy—whether you'll sell or rent. It outlines your firm's target investment types—multi-family apartment housing, single-family homes, townhomes, tiny homes, and so on. And it sets boundaries for your firm's geographical investment area.

Your Buy Box helps you quickly and easily assess whether an opportunity is the right fit for your organization. It also reduces risk and maximizes profitability by aligning investment decisions with your firm's strategic goals and mission. Don't put your firm at risk by investing without a clearly defined Buy Box.

Who's on your dream team?

Every notable accomplishment in history was the summation of individuals collectively working together for a common goal. This is true for politics, sports, and it applies to the world of real estate investing, too. As an Institutional investor it's imperative you strategically choose partners who possess the values, experience, expertise, and resources that will make your investments a success. But how can you be sure you're choosing the right partners for your team?

To ensure your organization is choosing the right partners you must be diligent and ask the right questions. First, you must be certain a potential partner's values align with your firm's mission. If you're focusing on delivering affordable housing to low-to-moderate income residents, working with a custom luxury builder could cause friction and ultimately failure for a project. Be sure to ask your potential partners about their core values and who they desire to serve in the marketplace.

Secondly, you must have a firm understanding of your potential partner's real estate experience and expertise. You want a partner who can lift risk and responsibility off your plate, not add to it. Be sure you understand their strategic capabilities.

Questions to ask include:

- Can your prospective partner execute your acquisition strategy?
- Do they understand how to facilitate due diligence?
- Can they prepare deals for title exchange?

- Do they have the construction and operational experience and expertise to develop a parcel of land or re-develop an existing structure?
- Can they help with your disposition strategy?

You need to understand how a potential partner can help your team accomplish its goals. Failure to gain a true assessment of a partner's capabilities is sure to lead to misaligned expectations, frustration, and most importantly lackluster results.

You must also understand the resources a potential partner can bring to the table. Whether it's technology and systems, or human and financial capital, you must have an understanding of everything a potential partner can help with. Many times you'll find a prospective partner who uses technology or vendors that could help save time and money—both critical pieces to a successful project. Or you might find a potential partner who has relationships that can make navigating challenges, like re-zoning approvals, a walk in the park. Be sure you understand all the resources a potential partner brings to your team.

Nothing spectacular is accomplished without a spectacular team. Be sure you've assessed the areas your firm needs help and look to bring on partners who possess the values, skill set, and resources that will help your institutional investment firm reduce risk and maximize profitability for all parties involved.

Are your systems leading you to success?

Investing in real estate can be tricky, to say the least. It's one thing to get lucky with an investment, but it's something totally different to produce profitable investments with low risk systematically and repeatedly. Stakeholders desire consistent results, which ultimately means consistent profits. But how can you provide consistency within your organization while providing consistent results for those your organization serves?

Having defined systems within an organization will provide the dependability all stakeholders desire, from employees to management, to clients and customers and investors. Systems lead to your success. But what systems do you need within your institutional investment firm to lead to the success you desire?

Today's business landscape has empowered small to large businesses with affordable software solutions that can be used to manage an entire business, from sales to operations and everything in between. One solution that comes to mind is Zoho One. This platform could allow your investment firm to move from multiple applications to one integrated business operating system with one login per user. Identifying software solutions that can help your team save time, money, and provide transparency across business functions is critical to your operational success.

Not all successful systems require coding, programming, and learning how to use complicated software applications. Many functions within your investment organization can be governed by a simple checklist. Checklists provide guidance for everyday tasks and allow management to on-board new members and partners, quickly and easily. Without a checklist, someone or a group of people have to "house" all necessary tasks and functions in their head, or at best on a sticky note. Using a checklist for each important area of your business will help save time, money, and most importantly frustration from missed tasks.

One of the most important systems you'll need to establish within your firm is organized communication. I'm not talking about telephone systems and email providers, although these are also important. I'm talking about how communication is facilitated and systematized across various functions of your firm.

Does your Acquisitions team meet weekly, monthly, or quarterly? Are the notes from the meeting stored and shared electronically so all parties can later access?

Are you meeting with investors on pre-determined intervals so they don't have to reach out to you with questions about projects and returns?

How often are you meeting with team members and partners to debrief and allow the opportunity for dialogue that may not be comfortably shared in large group settings?

By consistently and systematically communicating with all parties, you'll ensure your entire team feels heard and is vested in the success and mission of your organization.

Choosing not to set aside time to create systems for your business will lead to confusion, disappointment, and potentially failure. Don't allow this to happen. Schedule time today to begin creating the necessary systems and communication channels your investment firm needs in order to be successful today, and beyond.

Are you missing opportunities in plain sight?

Today's real estate market is hyper-competitive, and by the laws of nature, land supply will continue to dwindle. Multinational REITs (Real Estate Investment Trusts), private equity firms, and mom-and-pop investors are scouring the earth looking for redevelopment and raw land opportunities. As an institutional investor looking to supply consumer demand with maximum shareholder returns, you must begin to ask yourself two important questions. First, where is the next deal coming from? Second, how can we identify opportunities our competitors don't see?

While I was a budding entrepreneur, a mentor provided me with a great piece of advice: "Be a big fish in a small pond." How does that apply to real estate investing? It's easy. Look for small, nimble projects that others may deem too small, yet which could still provide healthy returns for your firm.

As an example, a client who's a non-profit institutional investment firm asked my partner and I to locate parcels of land that could be developed into single-family housing stock—either townhomes or single-family dwellings. While driving, my partner identified a small parcel of commercial land that had been on the market for almost two years. A person looking for land to build residential stock might keep moving... but not us. By understanding municipal zoning rules which allowed for commercial parcels to be used for multi-family housing stock (including townhomes), and knowing how to negotiate win-win deals, my partner and I were able to secure that parcel of land for our client to use to build townhomes.

Having the right expertise on your team can allow your firm to capitalize on investment opportunities others don't have the talent to see. The above-mentioned example yielded 10 townhome lots for our client, at a fraction of the cost the seller could have commanded if they understood zoning within their municipality. Other investors missed the opportunity because they weren't looking through the right lens. Don't be like other investors, look for opportunities in your market that others fail to see in plain sight.

Are you overpaying for lackluster investments?

Not overpaying for investments may seem like common sense. Unfortunately, over the years I've learned common sense ain't so common in the world of real estate! Investors, big and small alike, routinely over-pay for investment opportunities for two simple reasons. First, they want/need to do deals in order to keep investors happy. Or they've failed to complete proper due diligence prior to the transfer of title. It's that simple.

Need an example? Just look at the rise and fall of the Zillow iBuying machine. Zillow was on a tear for several years, purchasing single-family houses, doing minor renovations, and flipping for a profit. Then all of a sudden during the Covid-19 pandemic Zillow's iBuying monster came to a screeching halt. Zillow realized it couldn't profitably flip large numbers of investment properties. They stated the decision to discontinue iBuying wasn't based on market conditions but on an inability to manage inventory of homes needing renovations before being sold. The reality was that Zillow purchased too many bad deals because its model relied on purchases... not *profitable* purchases.

When you're focused on making low-risk investments that profitably fit your Buy Box, you'll do fewer deals yet remain profitable. And most importantly, you'll remain in business.

When your team is evaluating deals, be sure everyone uses a conservative valuation of the project's as-is value. Also be sure everyone uses conservative estimates of the end product's value. Do not be afraid to be conservative when evaluating costs and profitability of a project. Doing so provides your firm with two things: 1) If your estimates are low, the project will be more profitable in the long-term; 2) If the values of the end product end up being lower than estimated or the costs end up being more than anticipated, you've already accounted for these unknowns by being conservative in your valuation and cost estimates.

Don't allow your firm's hard work to go flying out the window because it's "sexy" to do a deal. Remember, the "deal of a lifetime" comes around about once a week. Or maybe it's once a month, or once a year. It won't matter if you miss a deal or two because you've chosen to be conservative. What matters most is your firm's ability to consistently do profitable deals that minimize risk and maximize the probability of profit. Overpaying for lackluster deals will never get your firm to its desired goals.

The world of institutional investing can be exciting, fun, and profitable. But only if you make sure you're following your team's plan. That means you're focused on investments that fall within your firm's Buy Box, you're strategic about who is on your team, you use systems that allow you to leverage success easily, you look for opportunities in plain sight that no one else sees, and you make sure you never overpay!

BUYER'S MINDSET

WITH *RAWLINS GOLDSTON*

RAWLINS GOLDSTON is a strong advocate of customer service. As someone with almost a decade of sales experience to his credit, he believes you cannot put a price on an amazing customer experience just as you can't trace back its unquantifiable returns.

During his free time, he likes to connect with his Instagram followers, bring them up to speed on his latest transactions, and share his love of food and cars.

Founder of Dallas Contemporary Homes, Rawlins believes in the power of simplicity, and so he channels his endless enthusiasm for contemporary homes, innovation, affordability, and customer service into crafting a model for like-minded individuals. In doing so, this sales expert has discovered a niche within a competitive market.

dallascontemporaryhomes.com
rawlins@dallascontemporaryhomes.com
(903) 664-5908

BUYER'S MINDSET

When it comes to buying a home, unfortunately, everyone tends to do the same things. Consequently, the very large majority of consumers get the same results. While this may be great in many ways, when it comes to real estate, the most savvy buyers *want* to get different results than the masses. The problem is many of them don't even realize that they *can* separate themselves from the market. Those buyers who do realize there is something better out there for themselves don't really know *how* to actually obtain it in an extremely competitive market.

Are you the buyer who wants to get the same deal that everyone else you know got (meaning endless searching, placing multiple offers, and waiving all your rights as a buyer), or are you the buyer who wants to take a different approach to your home shopping process?

Conventional wisdom tends to follow the process of jumping on the internet, looking at houses, then reaching out to go see a few that catch your attention with random real estate agents. In times when the market is somewhat balanced and buyer friendly, this flawed approach manages to function fairly well on the surface. However, when the market is tough and favorable for sellers, this same approach leaves many buyers feeling hopeless and without a plan for success other than spending exorbitant amounts of cash to waive appraisals and cover "over asking price" offers.

The aforementioned methodology often leads to buyer remorse right away for those who do buy, or it leads to total burnout for those who try and fail a few times. Imagine putting your best effort forward numerous times only to continuously miss every home you try for. That's what many buyers are experiencing in today's seller's market.

If you've read this far, it's probably safe to assume that you are either a buyer who has experienced this agony and wonders could've been done differently to avoid such an outcome, or you're a buyer who wants to avoid being another statistic altogether.

There's great news for you, and I'm excited to help you as a buyer see that there is a huge opportunity to adjust your thinking—before, during, and after buying a home! By simply doing things that others *aren't* doing and using this proven handful of strategies, you too can be wildly successful buying in any market and in any location.

Expectations

Over the years, I have worked with many buyers throughout extremely competitive contemporary homes real estate market in Dallas, Texas, and have seen the differentiators in how they approach the process and where their mindsets ultimately lay.

Buyers who are more open-minded get better deals in faster time and with less drama, nearly every time. In fact, first-time buyers tend to get the best deals, because they don't come into the process with so many preconceived notions of how things should go based on the last time they purchased.

If it's been more than 5-7 years since you've purchased your home, then throw most of the knowledge and tactics you used out of the window when approaching your next transaction. You'll save yourself and your agent a lot of unneeded stress!

So, what can *you* do to get the results you want? What can you change if your financials are already maxed out?

The fantastic news, is this won't cost you additional money. In fact, when done correctly, it should *save* you money!

The number one key to having success as a buyer is by developing the right set of expectations. As a buyer, you're far more capable of getting things done than you may realize. The problem is most buyers tend to follow what they think other buyers are doing. The result is a ton of buyers piling on top of one other to go after a very limited number of "hot" homes. By adjusting your expectations up front, you are likely to find that there are other opportunities that are just as desirable that are available to you without all the drama.

People want what other people want, and this fact shows itself time and again in the real estate market. If you're a seller, and the market is loaded with more buyers than homes for sale, then you're in a fantastic position. However, if you're a buyer, then a market heavily favoring sellers is working strongly against you. In a strong seller's market, buyers often pay significantly over asking price and basically give away all their rights while simultaneously looking at 20-50 homes and placing multiple offers hoping to get lucky and have one be accepted.

In some cases, buyers waive home inspections and option periods simply to "secure the deal." While the excitement of "winning the contract" may feel great, it's often not worth the risks and disadvantages associated with waiving the very rights that protect you as a buyer.

All the talk of there being "no inventory available," "everything selling way above asking price," and worrying about interest rates creates a panic mindset among buyers. Once you buy into that panic mindset, you've basically giving yourself permission to accept "fate." And when your expectations are based on overarching market rumors and stereotypes, then you're highly likely to act in a certain way that will produce an undesirable outcome.

So, if "doing what everyone is doing" is the mindset to avoid, then what's the one to embrace? If you follow the template that I'm about to describe for you, then you will not only avoid being another victim of the market, but you'll very likely find a home that you love, save a lot of money, and do it with minimal drama.

This is the exact framework for success that we use to help numerous clients of Dallas Contemporary Homes to dominate our contemporary and modern homes real estate market. The same concepts can be used anywhere there are homes being bought and sold; these concepts are not location specific.

Step One
Recognize that you're only buying one house. Market data, momentum, and opportunity risk aren't likely to be true across the market as a whole. Do your best to remove emotion from the equation, and don't get too attached to any one home. If you recognize that and address it, then you can create a wildly better result than the average buyer.

Step Two

Be prepared and speak with a quality *local* lender *before* you begin looking at homes. The average buyer doesn't even think about talking to a lender, until much later in the home search process. Unfortunately, many real estate agents don't tell buyers any better, and this ends up making the process significantly more difficult for them in the long run.

The primary problem buyers run into is not competition for quality homes, it's actually this financial aspect. You may expect that you're going to be able to spend a certain amount of money on a monthly payment, but by the time you add in escrows and taxes, the amount of home that number buys will be significantly different. Suddenly you realize the home you fell in love with is way outside of your budget.

You really don't want to discover this reality after you've been under contract on a home for a week. At that point you'll be pushing the limits of your financing contingency and risking your family's welfare. Knowing (not guessing) your financials is probably the single most powerful confidence and peace of mind builder for a buyer. Don't delay getting pre-approved; it will save you so much stress throughout the duration of the home search process.

Step Three

Determine your "must haves," "would like to haves," and your "not that big of a deal" aspects of a home. Your goal is to get 90% of what you *need*, 70% of what you *want*, and maybe 30% of the "I'm okay with or without it" features.

Remember, your job is to be as emotionally detached from each home as possible. Emotion is what drives buyers to do very crazy things in a market. By sticking to this formula, you will view each home in a far more objective manner, putting you eons ahead of most buyers in your local market.

Step Four
Use the internet for the powerful information tool that it is. Once upon a time, buyers checked out a few websites, made lists of homes they liked, and drove around for days trying to look at the houses in person. Many buyers had Realtors, but many chose to go at it alone.

"Winging it" used to be *the way*. Actually, "winging it" is still the way—to lots of wasted time, energy, money, and tons of frustration. The savviest buyers understand that the vast majority of information they need to know about a home is readily available right from their computer or smart phone. Why spend hours driving around looking at homes that a quick web search would've easily disqualified?

You'd be surprised how many people still utilize this outdated approach. Those are also the same people who are having very little success in the buying market. The internet (MLS portals particularly) is one of the strongest tools in your arsenal. Use it to your advantage.

Step Five
When you're ready to start making offers, set very clear boundaries on what you are willing to do and not do. This is likely a recurring theme to you by now, but in case it's not, here's one final reminder: *Avoid* becoming overly emotional during the buying process. This principle holds especially true when it comes to writing offers.

Each of the previous four steps should be working in unison to help you breeze through the offer process. If you've followed the framework correctly, then you'll be very dialed into the type of home you're looking for, you'll know exactly what your budget is, and you'll also know where you're able and willing to compromise and where you're not.

The sum of all these parts is an extremely prepared buyer who is not only willing and able to buy, but also is *ready* to buy. There are plenty of other buyers in the market who are willing and able, but few are actually *ready*, willing, and able.

You cannot truly be ready until you've done the prep-work, and as you've learned by this point, that's just not many people. That's why they jump into the fast pace of the market, and find themselves being swept up in its current. This won't be you, because you now have a foolproof formula, framework, and strategy to get out there and make your own pathway to home buying success instead of taking whatever the market gives you.

Don't follow conventional wisdom if you expect to get different results for yourself. You must be willing to think outside the box and go against the status quo. It's not about speed. Instead, it's about research and preparedness. Your mindset and approach and preparation upfront will place you in a far stronger buying position, and that will ultimately help to ensure that you get a wonderful deal on a home you'll love for many years to come!

BUYING LIKE A CELEBRITY

WITH BRIAN WITT

BRIAN WITT was born and raised in beautiful Bozeman, MT. His family roots extend six generations through Montana soil. With that type of family legacy, he is deeply committed to preserving what makes Montana special while also looking to the future.

As a third-generation Realtor his family has dedicated their lives to serving others. They have persisted through 12 recessions, watched the state's economy change from a heavy mining/industry and agricultural production, to becoming a prime relocation state and leader in tourism. They not only understand Montana history deeply but, more importantly, know its future better than anyone else.

Their clients have been with them through first home purchases, second home purchases, the purchasing of their first investment properties, development projects, and the passing of real estate assets to second and third generations. They are truly dedicated to serving you for life.

www.bison-realty.com
brian@bison-realty.com
(406) 285-8546

BUYING LIKE A CELEBRITY

Most people assume only celebrities get to enjoy the home buying experience differently, but once you understand the incredible possibilities, it just might change your life.

Buying like a celebrity means you've attained a point in your life that enables you to purchase properties no matter where they are, simply because you want to. They don't necessarily have to check a box for what your family needs, like in terms of the number of bedrooms and bathrooms or attached garages. You may just be buying this property for a one-week stay or an entire year, but you want to have exclusive accommodations that are luxurious. Or maybe you're interested in a property with a large amount of land so you cannot even see the lights of the next closest home. Maybe you want a place nearby to unique nightlife, or that has complete privacy, or majestic views.

If you're accustomed to operating in a diligent, logical, family-oriented way, this concept will likely seem foreign, but so-called normal people really can own incredible homes with exclusivity and privacy in gorgeous places, with unique nightlife opportunities where they can escape their everyday burdens and obligations.

Maybe you're attracted to the idea of celebrity ownership, but never really felt like it was approachable. If that's the case, here's what you need to know to realistically consider this incredible opportunity.

What is it about the celebrity lifestyle that attracts you? Maybe it's because you want to have anonymity in a small town. Or maybe you enjoy going out to eat at the best bars and restaurants. Are you a fan of absolute luxury and world-class experiences? How about being able to walk out your front door and start skiing, fishing, hiking, or engaging in your favorite outdoor activities?

It could even be shopping or attending festivals. Whatever "celebrity living" means for you, it also equates with you having complete control over your environment. For example, if you're only going to visit the property a couple of weeks each year, you can still have everything be exactly the way you want. No hotel room or VRBO will ever fulfill all your exact passions the same way.

Our family office has worked with a billionaire client who decided to purchase a house that was down the street from their own home. They wanted a nice place where a friend could stay, because she absolutely didn't want the friend to live with her.

This might seem extreme and out of reach, but consider what it might look and feel like to be able to purchase a separate property where your friends or family could stay when they come to town to visit. A celebrity lifestyle can be achieved on many kinds of budgets, because it's actually all about the celebrity mindset.

The first step to making this a reality is to decide which aspects of celebrity property ownership are attractive to you. If you're most drawn to privacy and exclusivity, then you want to start looking into markets that have gated communities or places with lots of land.

If instead you're drawn to being in the public eye and experiencing incredible nightlife, then this points to certain locations that make this possible.

For those who love the energy of movies or media festivals, investigate not only the overall markets but also the communities around properties that can provide that within a reasonable travel distance.

Maybe your interest in this lifestyle is so you can gain complete control of the environment. In this case you're going to want to look for standalone properties in communities where there is an established sense that locals and other visitors respect private property.

Next let's identify financial parameters for your desired celebrity lifestyle.

Can you use this property for investment purposes? In these cases you will want to look for a property that will appreciate over time, or that can help pay for itself as a short-term rental. You don't want to be in a costly location like Park City, Utah, or Vail, Colorado, which have already been tapped and where market prices have skyrocketed. Look for markets that have big growth potential in the near future.

Is your buying approach for diversification purposes? In this case you might prefer the stability of owning a large ranch over trading privately held companies on the stock market which can swing wildly in a day.

Maybe you'd like to create a legacy property for your family, setting up an asset for future generations. For some, that can mean purchasing a log cabin in the mountains that will be shared with family and friends. For others it is a lake property with a primary home and a boathouse with rooms for guests—or wild teenagers. Other families purchase ski-in/ski-out properties to go on multifamily generational ski trips every year. Some families buy property with hundreds of acres in prime hunting grounds and maintain farm or ranch operations to help offset the cost of ownership—even setting up guided hunts as a means of additional revenue and a chance to share their land with others who share the same passions.

However, if this purchase is because you've attained so much success in your profession that it literally won't change your financial outlook, then you need to give yourself permission to remove all caps and limits and really go for it. This property can just be for sheer fun!

Once you've established the answers to these questions, it's time to investigate and gain familiarity with specific markets and potentially make a site visit.

How do you gain familiarity in a marketplace? The first and probably best way is to visit that location. Go spend a week or two vacationing in the area. Or you could read about the location in travel magazines or online travel guides.

If you have particular hobbies or interests, there are always "Top 10" lists like "Top 10 Dog-friendly Towns" that will provide you with extra information and some insider peeks into the communities.

You will definitely want to connect with a seasoned professional realtor who can take care of all the details for you. For example, a lot of our clientele interested in the Bozeman market will fly in for a weekend to narrow the properties and place an offer, or even potentially buy from a distance and make their first visit one where they get to enjoy the property.

It's certainly possible to do the digging on your own. If you have a friend who already lives in the location you're interested in, consider asking them for insight and tips. A professional agent does this on a regular basis and can help you ask all the right questions and investigate the right options and experiences for you.

Finally, it's time to quit dreaming and take action. Once you've identified your desired celebrity lifestyle and financial approach, and found a world-class realtor in the area to help, it's time to make the magic happen.

The last thing you would ever want to do is go through all that work only to stall out at the best part, especially if you're looking for properties that will appreciate considerably. For example the Big Sky, Montana, real estate market is up 100% over prices last year. And there's still room for growth. This is not a situation where you will benefit by sitting on the fence for 3-6 months or even more. In a rapidly appreciating market, you could lose 15-20% by waiting to take action on the exact same property.

The best advice I can give you is to take action and begin to experience the lifestyle and investment opportunities that you've been dreaming of.

We recently had a buyer from Los Angeles who did his homework online, called us, then bought a property sight-unseen four days later. Another flew in for the weekend and bought their property after spending an afternoon touring the home and surrounding grounds. With a solid on-the-ground agent, you can confirm the images you see online with a live tour of the home through simple technology like Zoom or FaceTime.

If you're interested in an area where market conditions can change exponentially, don't delay experiencing this dream. It can cost time and money, but more than anything, it costs a gap in the dream. Every day you delay is a day you won't have over again. If you're ready for a unique property, likely other people are searching for it too. And when that home comes onto the market, it's going to be snatched up and may not ever come back on the market again during your lifetime.

You've made it so far in this amazing life. Isn't it time you started enjoying the benefits of celebrity ownership?

BUILDING YOUR WATERFRONT TIMELINE

WITH STEPHANIE JONES

Having grown up vacationing with her family on Burt Lake in Northern Michigan, **STEPHANIE JONES** formed a love of water at an early age. After relocating from Metro Detroit to the vacation paradise that is Northern Michigan, Stephanie decided it was time to embark on a new career. Drawing from her experience as a business person and entrepreneur, she decided real estate would be the best fit considering the incredible properties available and unforgettable family experiences she could help provide to clients. Stephanie and her team work every day to ensure her clients receive unparalleled levels of professional service. Stephanie lives with her husband and two children in the heart of Northern Michigan.

**www.jonesnorth.com
stephanie@jonesnorth.com
(231) 844-4410**

BUILDING YOUR WATERFRONT TIMELINE

There are two truths that I encounter almost daily in my career as a real estate broker: there is never enough time... or waterfront real estate! In the following chapter I discuss the importance of efficiency and a condensed timeframe, and why they are of the utmost importance when negotiating and ultimately acquiring your waterfront dream home.

Typically when working with clients on a waterfront home purchase, it is for a second home or vacation property. I work with everyone from young singles to couples looking for an escape in retirement. With all of my clients, setting the initial expectation accurately helps cut down on a lot of heartache and unnecessary time-waste later in the purchase process.

In our initial consultation, it is important to me to understand your motivation and discover what you are truly looking for when selecting a waterfront property. I want to know your connection with the place and what motivates you to make the jump to ownership.

Having a good idea of what you actually want and need is important before you begin your search. Waterfront markets are extremely competitive and homes do not linger, regardless of the current economy. This is especially true in our post-pandemic world. Depending on where you're located, knowing whether you will use the property only in summer, all year round, or also on the shoulder seasons will help refine your search, as some homes are not designed for year-round use.

Another aspect of waterfront ownership that is important to understand is your available amenities, or *access* to those amenities. Are you looking for a resort lifestyle with nearby shopping, or do you want more of a rural escape to be close to nature for solitude and peace? Before you begin your search, consider which amenities outside the home itself are important to you and your family.

What makes purchasing on the waterfront unique

There are many things that come into play when purchasing a home on the waterfront that do not apply to traditional residential homes. The distance of the home to the water, building codes, grandfathered building codes, and what happens to the waste from the home are all unique to life on the water. Also, local municipalities and neighbors tend to be significantly more sensitive to a home's impact on the environment, especially when dealing with aspects that could potentially affect the health of a lake or other water source.

In some waterfront communities, even the type of vegetation you choose to plant and where you plant it is closely regulated and policed by neighborhood associations and government agencies. Your local expert realtor should know this information, or at least know exactly where to find it, so you can understand exactly what to expect.

I have past clients who came to me for help after they purchased a magnificent home on a golf course without truly understanding everything involved in that community. What they were not prepared for was the parade of maintenance people, designers, cleaning staff, gardeners, and other trades that were required for the home just to exist. What they really wanted was a low-maintenance place to get away from the hustle and bustle so they could relax with friends and family. Ultimately, we ended up selling that home and getting them a spectacular condominium with a tranquil view over a lake.

While you might picture yourself using a property just on the holidays at first, it's important to think through to the future if this property may be something you eventually want to use year-round. Is the home somewhere your family would be willing to come visit? Is it convenient for access to the kinds of activities to make the memories you envision?

There are many details when purchasing a vacation home on the water that you may not be prepared for that a local adviser can educate you about, such as property taxes, resort fees, homeowner association fees, tourist taxes, and rental restrictions. The latter is particularly important if you plan to offset ownership expenses with short-term rentals through an online platform. More and more areas are severely restricting a homeowner's ability to do this. It could be financially devastating to purchase a property outside of your budget in the hope of offsetting expenses through rentals only to find out after the fact that it is not allowed.

Getting ready

As you begin your home search for a waterfront property, there are few things you should have in place beforehand. Will you be financing or paying cash? Are you able to sign for and execute all purchase decisions? Or is it necessary to have a trustee, lawyer, or banker involved? Getting these people on board beforehand will be important, as a prolonged negotiation or delay in processing paperwork could potentially kill a deal.

I've had multiple deals fall apart due to illness, change of job, divorce, or other things that influenced the timeframe of closing. Getting the deal under contract and closed fast, prevents you from these unforeseen risks.

On the topic of lending, many of my clients already have a relationship with their local mortgage officer or personal banker. While this is fantastic and may have worked well in your primary marketplace, it can be tricky in a different state, or even country. Depending on the way property is zoned, it can affect a bank's ability to extend a loan on it. Working with a local adviser who is aware of competitive banks that have provided mortgages in a specific area to previous clients is extremely helpful and can move the process along dramatically.

A local real estate professional is like a specialty matchmaker who knows exactly what you're looking for and the unique characteristics within the marketplace that make certain properties most exciting for you. Occasionally in some waterfront markets there will be many homes to choose from, but wouldn't you rather enjoy spending your time getting to know one community that somebody else has vetted, saving you from racing around looking at every prospective property on the market and researching the surrounding area? Investing time up front to work with a real pro will make touring properties significantly more efficient and faster.

Seasonality

Another thing to keep in mind when purchasing a waterfront home is the time of year when you want to take possession. If you are looking for a summer home, the purchase process could take 30, 60, or even 90 days to close, depending on factors such as inspection, permits, remodeling, appraisals and loan closure. Because of this, if you haven't planned far enough in advance, you could lose an entire season—putting you back one whole year from enjoying your new purchase!

In Northern climates, the second home or waterfront properties typically see the most closings from September through November. Does that surprise you? Generally people like to visit the area and vacation during the summer. This helps to narrow down where they would like to be. Also, many families like to get one last holiday season out of a waterfront property before listing it at the end of a season, so many properties in this situation enter the market in the autumn.

With the help of a local expert, you can speed up your time investment. The best realtors know about off-market properties, or that one seller who's been waiting for the perfect buyer, or even that property that hasn't been available for 35 years... but everyone on the coastline knows it's a rare six-bedroom home where no others exist.

Wouldn't it be great to get to town and have your dream home under contract before dinner? To make that happen, let's be really clear. When you understand your approach, your on-the-ground expert can hand-select a few, maybe three, properties for you to view. You'll already know that each of them would be perfect for your needs, but you'll have the ability to pick from the best of the best because they have been vetted for you.

The typical buyer for this type of property who wants to move quickly is generally flying in or visiting for a short time. Prior to arrival, I structure the agenda for our entire day, from airport transportation to coordinating our meetings. I assemble all the documentation in a welcome packet so you have something to hold onto and reference while touring homes that have been prepared for your viewing and on which I've educated myself ahead of time.

This way when I take you on a tour, I have a sound knowledge base to answer many of your questions without having to research or call other people. I'm also able to plan our route between the homes if you'd like to stop for lunch or coffee or to meet with third parties like builders or designers, or to visit nearby docks or rental management agencies. I line up all of those meetings and provide you with introductions to preferred vendors and suppliers that I've worked with in the past, so you don't have to do the research to know you're working with reputable referrals. You could burn up a lot of time and money hiring the wrong people to work in and around your new dream home!

These days, technology has been a huge benefit to people who are purchasing a home from out of town. With the advent of virtual reality tours, digital measurement tools, and electronic forms and signatures, most of what used to take place in person can now be handled remotely. By using virtual home tours and 3D scanning, I can send accurate digital measurements and floor plans so you and your family, designer, contractor or architect can begin customizing your new property from the comfort of home without making multiple trips out of town. Also during the negotiations and financing process, many forms must be sent back and forth for signatures. This can now be done anywhere from your phone or tablet, saving an immense amount of time and energy.

Bringing it together

Ultimately, the goal of this entire process is about your time. It's about how you want to spend the finite amount of time you have on this Earth. Making the decision about who you want to be with and where you want to be with them may be one of the most important and lasting decisions you ever make.

I strive everyday to ensure that people are spending time with their loved ones in a magnificent place and not wasting too much energy on the technicalities of the home search and buying process.

Time can either kill deals or make them happen. If you are able to move quickly with a sound knowledge base and a trusted advisor on your side, purchasing a home on the waterfront can be done quickly and painlessly.

In the end, there are no better moments than those created with friends and family enjoying time together at an amazing escape!

BUILDING WEALTH THROUGH REAL ESTATE

WITH MATTHEW PATTERSON

Born and raised in rural Indiana, **MATTHEW PATTERSON** began his entrepreneurial journey in his late teens. Brought up by parents who both ran small businesses, he followed in their footsteps and built his own asphalt paving company. With long hours, dedication, and plenty of hard work, he created a successful business that he led for 14 years. In 2005, he moved to sunny Southwest Florida to start a new career path in Real Estate and went fulltime in 2011. About 5 years in, he attended a Keller Williams Mega Camp event where he learned about their culture and vision of the company which encompassed everything he believed in: God, family, and then business.

He began as a single thriving agent but needed help to ensure he was able to provide the best experience for his clients. He added an assistant and from there has built a team of 15 known as The Patterson Group. Matthew has an extensive investing portfolio—purchasing, holding, and selling rental properties. His knowledge and experience benefit many of his clients, as he can provide them with honest and trustworthy advice.

When he isn't breaking records with more than 400 SOLD properties in 2021, leading his team with strong leadership, hosting his weekly radio show "Real Estate Exposed," attending speaking engagements, and everything else in between, he is a devoted husband and father. Married to his lovely wife, Nikki, and father to ever-joyful daughter Everly who is the absolute apple of his eye, he consistently strives to provide the best life for them. An avid hunter, lover of boating, and anything to do with heavy machinery, he feels extremely blessed.

www.MatthewPatterson.com
Matthew@PattersonGroupKW.com
(941) 621-8600 (office)
(941) 375-1312 (cell)

BUILDING WEALTH THROUGH REAL ESTATE

My entire life, my parents taught that preparing and planning for financial stability and security were essential. The number one asset they spoke to me about was the home.

"There's no greater asset," they told me, and at that time, the average annual increase in value was around 4%. Skip ahead to 2007 and The Great Recession. We all remember the terrible bust, after the boom before it saw price increases up 300% in some markets. Regardless of the real estate market or state of the economy, the one thing you cannot do is neglect your home.

I've walked in to many properties where the owners were not even able to recoup the cost of their home purchase because they had neglected to maintain the property through normal wear and tear. Their lack of upkeep was the direct cause of their home's depreciation in value.

When thinking about annual appreciation, it's important to consider the cashflow element. In general, regular maintenance is required, even for short-term investments.

Buying for your primary residence

I bought my first home at age 19, because of my parents' influence, but I had already been managing their 14 rentals. This opened my eyes to the differences between renting and buying. Renters have the benefit of not needing to deal with repairs, while homeowners know that routine maintenance is the key to preserving their investment.

Even if you don't think of yourself as an investor, you will benefit from allowing the concept of wealth building to factor into your decision-making in the purchase of a home.

If you look at your annual budget for what it takes to live, imagine if you owned your home outright. What would that do for your life? What would that do for your children? What would that do for your ability to travel? For healthcare inevitabilities? Would you continue to work? Of course there will still be taxes and insurance, but for most people, owning their own home equals freedom. It gives them options.

When I talk with home buyers these days, they can easily get distracted by the emotion of buying a home. It is natural to envision your children and family dinners, holiday gatherings, and all the experiences that take place in a beloved house.

However, bear in mind that investment properties will likely not be the same kind of house you're going to live in. It comes down to ROI (return on investment) and location.

Even if your primary motivation for buying a property is for personal residence, it will pay off to consider the wealth-building aspects as they can help you make better choices around cash vs. financing, location, features, and timing.

Also consider that every home doesn't have to be your "forever home." Many people are ready to move in five years or less because conditions in their life have evolved. Just since the start of the pandemic, investors with large portfolios have begun selling their properties because they decided to take early retirement.

Those who rented from these investors are now on the phone with realtors, distraught. "I just was given 30-day notice and I've got to be out. The lease is up and they're selling my house."

For the investor, the huge rise in property value is a boon. But for the renter who is out there working hard and has a budget, a home that went from a $1300 per month rental cost to $2,600 per month as a mortgage has just killed their financial plan. They're having a hard time finding a place to live and often wind up relocating to other parts of the country.

Buying rental properties

If I'm investment minded and being very deliberate about wanting to make money, the most approachable way is to garner a professional Realtor who is plugged into the market. This expert comes with knowledge and experience of what equates to short-term and long-term real estate gains.

When accruing wealth from real estate, it's imperative to get the timing right. With time, everything else is on your side. In the past, I may have paid 5% more on a $100,000 home because I saw the market and knew what was going on. That 5% was trivial because I gained 50% in the next 12-18 months. When you don't personally have that level of insight into market trends and shifts, you need someone on your side who brings the benefit of specialized knowledge.

Most people have been a renter at one point or another, but still have limited understanding of being an owner... or being a landlord, which can have negative connotations. But there is a way to do it right and a way to do it wrong. If your goal is to build wealth, one tip is to thoroughly check out a property and know what you're buying. Have a home inspection, and never try to save a few hundred when it could cost you tens of thousands later.

Some people mistakenly assume that when a property's mortgage is paid off, they get to keep $X amount each month. I'm a huge fan of rentals, but you need to look at something called "carrying cost." This is the true cost to carry that property, maintain it, and keep it in working order. Only when you have a clear picture of the carrying cost can you accurately estimate your net profit on a per month basis.

A lot depends on your goals. If you know you need to make $X amount of profit within a certain timeframe, then you shouldn't buy a rental that won't have immediate positive cashflow. You also don't want to speculate on the short-term because the market jumps and drops dramatically.

From there, determine what you want your portfolio to look like in the long term. Examine trends and cycles, as well as geographical considerations. Things are very different in the Midwest than Florida. Night and day. Is it better to invest in properties where you live, or in a different portion of the country?

Another strategy to consider is knowing how long you intend to hold a property. If you have intend to hold a home for about 10 years, but the roof will need to be replaced in 8, then you need to factor in the replacement cost. At the same time, consider the wiring, septic systems, and air-conditioning. Those are all big expenses that should be calculated into every home you buy.

When you calculate your cashflow, you need to factor in some deferred maintenance. The reason for this is if you're only making $80 bucks a month, you likely won't make any profit because you're going to have to spend that money every year on upkeep.

Almost every property will have at least $1,000 in annual repairs. And over the long-term, you're going to need to replace a water heater, A/C, the furnace, the roof, and maybe some windows. Whatever the case, if your margins are too thin, appreciation is the only way the property will help you accumulate wealth. And appreciation is never guaranteed. In a case like this, one major repair can wipe out your profitability for the whole year.

The number one thing people neglect to factor in is vacancy. When a system is down for repair, or someone moves out, there will be lost time where the property will not generate cashflow. It's likely that you will lose 30 days in either of these instances, so you might as well budget for it in advance. I've even seen some lose 60 days.

Another common mistake I see regarding short-term holdings is not understanding the difference between rental properties and short-term rentals like seasonal or vacation properties. Additionally, you will have state tax that gets added in. In some states, that may be 12% on top of everything else.

When considering buying a property to list on Airbnb, VRBO, or the like, remember that these are usually furnished rental. Not just furniture, but also pots and pans, dishes, and decorations. That's another expense. Of course the rents are much higher, but you really need to calculate that ahead of time.

Also understand that vacancy and potential maintenance on short-term rentals is much different than regular rental units. When someone is living in the home longer, they generally take better care of the property than when they'll only be there for a week.

Short-term rental owners rarely factor in the increased management cost burden. With annual rentals, the property is turning over perhaps every 1-3 years. But with short-term rentals, you're turning it over every 2-3 days or once a week. Cleaning fees, restocking costs, and maintenance will be much higher. But just as the expenses are higher, so is the rental income and your risk due to market volatility.

Another oversight I see people make when investing in short-term rentals is they believe they're going to get a free vacation home. The problem is that you probably want to use the property during your biggest income opportunities. Seasonality can become a burden quickly.

Buying to "flip" a property

Another option is "flipping" which you may have enjoyed learning about on TV. At first it can feel overwhelming or out of reach but know that it's totally doable as well. And there are multiple ways to approach it.

The most important aspect of flipping is time. Every day is an expense. It used to be easier to locate contractors to help you, but now many of them are busy building houses. You will need to assemble your "dream team" of contractors who can swoop in on a project and dovetail to bring the renovations to completion.

Next, you need someone on your side who can price out exactly what it's going to take to renovate and flip the property. The wealth is usually made on the purchase price which enables you to sell for a profit. You need to have a buffer in there in case mid-renovation you discover a leaky septic tank or faulty water heater.

On top of your dream team of contractors, you will want to assemble a savvy Realtor and a good accountant.

Remember to calculate the cost of insurance. Some flippers choose to embrace the risk and not carry insurance. If you have a large portfolio and you have the funds to tolerate this risk, knowing it's not going to bankrupt you, then that's your choice. But for me, I like to have the security of knowing that I'm covered because anything can happen.

Remember that when you're flipping a home, the property is standing vacant. Other people realize it's vacant because they see the dumpsters and know what's happening. Make sure you are protected in the event of theft or damage.

Another thing to consider when budgeting the remodel is that this isn't the home you're planning to move your family into. As an investor, you need to see through the buyer's eyes. What will appeal to the masses? You may love pink or purple like my daughter, but don't paint the inside of your flips pink and purple.

I typically recommend going with a neutral color palette. I didn't say unattractive, I said neutral. This will allow more people to become interested in your property, which will help you get more money back when it's time to sell.

It's not about fashion. I know you could add a lot of extra things just because that's your taste and you love the way it looks but ask yourself whether it will make both dollars and "sense."

As an investor, also remember you've got to factor in the taxes. When you watch flips on TV they never ever show carrying costs or taxes as part of their profit. Don't get confused into believing that everything after the purchase price is pure profit.

Long-term flips

Another option is purchasing a property that you will make into your primary home for a set period of time, perhaps two years. That way you won't have capital gains issues.

For me, I do not purchase any flip property that I would not be okay with keeping if the market changes. That way, the home can shift in my portfolio to a longer-term holding and it doesn't break the bank. Remember not to purchase property using funds you need to buy the groceries. There is no guarantee. This is an investment and you want to operate out of abundance rather than scarcity which can cause you to make mistakes due to stress. When you have time and flexibility on your side, you can calmly negotiate the best deal. You will not have to take that first offer.

When it comes to owner-occupied long-term flips, one of the benefits is that you can always live in a remodeled home. You buy a house, remodel it, enjoy it for a couple of years, then sell it tax-free. Then you can do it again.

For other homeowners, that's not always the case because they're trying to stretch into the best home they can afford. With this strategy of slow flipping, you can quickly upgrade your personal home to a pretty unbelievable home, all with tax-free money.

If you're really focused on wealth building through real estate, we flip for big surges of cash, we hold for long-term wealth building, and we hold for cash flow. For example, I might flip a house once a year or every 2-3 years, but during the same amount of time I get into two or three rentals.

They can serve each other by mediating risk of operating only in one marketplace.

Some properties are better suited for rental than flipping and vice versa. The more comfortable you become with the different strategies, the easier it will be for you to take advantage of the best option to build wealth from the opportunities that present themselves.

As someone interested in building wealth through real estate, one or all of these strategies might be attractive. The really great thing about real estate is there are a lot of ways to build wealth. You may be drawn to only short-term rentals or only slow flips, but as you learn more about different approaches, you'll find increased opportunities. And the longer you do this, the more frequently you can turn a good deal into a great deal.

If you choose to pursue any one of those approaches, there is wealth to be built in real estate. You can do it one property at a time or more frequent. Many use a combination of these approaches. They flip homes for surges of cash that can be invested in more rental property for long-term slow and steady income as well as appreciation.

For those who want to build generational wealth, there is room on the spectrum for everyone, and it can be really exciting. My parents taught me so much about financial security and wealth building.

WHY RELATIONSHIPS MATTER

WITH DAVID GOSS

DAVID GOSS serves as a buyer specialist for the Todd Tramonte team where he specializes in serving buyers in his hometown of Richardson. There is not a street in Richardson David hasn't driven. He knows it like the back of his hand. It's this base of knowledge that makes him a great fit for anyone looking to make Richardson and the surrounding areas their home. His market knowledge and tenacity are beneficial to his clients in any area of the metroplex.

David is the quintessential team player, and his team-first mindset makes him invaluable to his family, his fellow team members, and his clients. He is a former collegiate athlete, and his competitive drive still shows up in how he fights for his clients on a daily basis. David has an earnest desire to provide world-class value. This care and concern shows through outside of his work. He has invested decades of faithful service into various local organizations, such as YoungLife and Fellowship of Christian Athletes, where he impacts the community in a manner that extends far beyond real estate.

David and wife Catha have a pair of children. His son Mason works alongside him as a member of the team. He is married to Ginny, and the couple made David a grandpa when they welcomed their daughter Lucy into the world. His daughter Kendall returned to DFW after graduating from Texas A&M University and works for Southwest Airlines.

www.toddtramonte.com
david@toddtramonte.com
214.995.4796 **(214) 995-4796**

WHY RELATIONSHIPS MATTER

In my experience with many buyers over the years, not every deal is just a transaction. It goes much deeper. Approaching buying a property without the mindset of having a relationship with your agent can be dangerous. Relationships are the backbone of real estate. It starts with you, but also includes relationships with the listing agent, the mortgage lender, the home inspector, the title company, and so on.

The list of key and important relationships is endless in real estate. But how can you, the buyer, establish all these connections on your own? You don't need to. Whether it's your heating and air-conditioning contact, the foundation guy, the roofer, or even a moving company, your real estate agent has important relationships in place that will work in your favor when buying or selling a home.

Sadly, many buyers do not want to invest the time in finding the right real estate agent to help them with one of the biggest decisions in life, to find an agent who has already built those relationships. Most buyers just want to go straight to the seller or sign up with the first agent they talk to, even without asking anything about the network of contacts and relationships that person brings to the table. Whether it's a buyer's market or a seller's market or a stable market, this shortsighted approach winds up hurting them.

They think it is all about the numbers, all about speed, and all about who's paying for what, but those deals are less likely to close and fund. It is also far less likely that both the buyer and seller will be happy with the outcome and feel like they got what they wanted.

These are the types of transactions that lead to buyer remorse, where unfortunately the home becomes a burden instead of a blessing. The approach, even before the buying process got started, set them up for failure.

My clients John Michael and Meredith Ruder had an area picked out that they wanted to buy in, but homes there rarely ever came up for sale. In fact, they'd looked at buying in that area for over five years. Finally, one popped up on the market and somebody else quickly put it under contract, but I knew the listing agent's son through my daughter, so I called her and said, "Hey, our kids know each other, and I have some clients who really want this house. What's it going to take to get the property?" We ended up working out that deal, and now John and Meredith have the home they always dreamed of—a couple acres in the middle of town with a pool—and they were able to remodel it just the way they envisioned and are thrilled to death.

With Jesse and Stacie Hensarling, they had a house sell, but not listed on the market yet. A home came on the market they loved and so we made an offer, but it was contingent on them selling their own home first. I quickly connected the listing agent with our team and with our mortgage lender so they would feel comfortable with negotiating a contingency sale. After these discussions, the listing agent quickly replied, "We will go with your offer!" The relationships I had built helped my clients win that deal and get the perfect property for their family.

My clients Bonnie and Earnest Curry were trying to figure out the three different air-conditioning systems on a townhouse they wanted to purchase. After I made a few phone calls and did some research, I learned that the guy who installed all the units was our same HVAC guy we have been working with for several years. Amazing! This relationship made the whole deal feel really comfortable because they got to talk to him before the purchase. It all came full circle with success for both the seller and buyer, because the last nail in that deal was all about the air conditioners.

My son Mason bought a house a couple of years ago, on the front end of the global pandemic. I knew the listing agent from a previous deal. I called her and asked about the property, but it had just gone under contract. She let me know the sale was likely to fall through, however, because the current buyer was having trouble getting a loan. I told her, "I'm sending you an offer right now." And we ended up executing the sale which turned out to be a perfect home for Mason. It worked out just because of that great relationship I'd built with the other agent.

Relationships are relevant in each type of market. Because my relationships give my clients an unfair advantage, I often have access to properties that aren't even on the market yet, that no one else would even know about, so I am able to get an offer accepted without it turning into a bidding war.

Normally a lender works, at best, 8:00 A.M. – 5:00 P.M., sitting in an office. When they turn off the computer and walk out the door, they cease to care about you. With contractors, they often don't answer or return calls until they need to line up new jobs. Title companies close promptly at 5:00 P.M. and likely shut off the phones off at 4:00. Listing agents usually are focused solely on obtaining their sellers the highest price. But when your realtor has built relationships—when they slow down to care and do a little research... making connections through their children or sports or college alumni, or a shared love of food or whatever—magical things can happen. Your buying process benefits.

How does this help you as the buyer? When you are picking a buyer agent, set up a consultation where you learn about the person before going out to look at homes. Give yourself that comfort of getting to know each other, and making sure they're a good fit for you. You want a skilled, experienced, world-class real estate agent. When you find this person, relationship building is something they already understand. I may be biased because this is what I do for home buyers in the Dallas/Fort Worth area, all day, every day. Typically folks come to me because they do not have their own massive network of longtime relationships with lenders, title companies, or contractors. As a buyer, you can shortcut the need to develop such a network by having access to it through a great real estate agent.

More than just at the time of sale, all those amazing benefits will be available to you while you are simply enjoying home ownership, when it comes time for repairs if there is a storm or insurance claim, or if the time comes down the road when you might want to sell and buy again.

Relationships matter. They just do. One of our team's core values is "Build relationships that you would be proud to tell your grandchildren about." That is what I focus on every day, building relationships that matter in my business and for my family and friends.

Made in the USA
Monee, IL
24 June 2022